SUPER DUPER TRIVIA BOOK

Volume 2

APPLESAUCE PRESS

KENNEBUNKPORT, MAINE

Applesauce press is an imprint of
Cider Mill Press Book Publishers
"Where good books are ready for press"
P.O. Box 454
12 Spring Street
Kennebunkport, ME 04046

Visit us online!
cidermillpress.com

Printed in China

1 2 3 4 5 6 7 8 9 0
First Edition

CONTENTS

CHAPTER 1

History

1. In 1565, Pedro Menendez founded which settlement in Florida, the oldest European settlement in the Americas?

a. Miami   b. Pascua Florida

c. Tampa   d. St. Augustine

2. What have archeologists found a lot of in the graves of East Coast Native Americans?

a. Weapons

b. Glass

c. European trade goods

d. Tobacco

3. True or false? By the 1650s, the Dutch colony of New Netherland hadn't attracted enough colonists to survive as a real colony.

Match the Revolutionary War battle with the side that won it:

4. Battle of Saratoga	a. British
5. Siege of Charleston	b. British
6. Battle of Yorktown	c. American colonies
7. Battle of Bunker Hill	d. British
8. Battle of White Plains	e. American colonies

Answers: 1. d; 2. c; 3. True; 4. c or e (American colonies) 5. a, b, or d (British); 6. c or e (American colonies); 7. a, b, or d (British); 8. a, b, or d (British)

9. Unlike Columbus, the explorer Amerigo Vespucci discovered which of these things?

a. That the Earth is round

b. That America was not part of Asia but was a new land

c. That the lands to the west were poor in natural resources

d. That Europe could benet from trade with the new lands

10. **True or false?** For the English-American colonies of the late seventeenth century, the king gave each colony to an individual, family, or group that he trusted.

11. TRUE OR FALSE? NEWSPAPERS, BOOKS, JOURNALS, AND PAMPHLETS WERE NOT EASILY AVAILABLE IN THE AMERICAN COLONIES.

12. The French explorer Samuel de Champlain founded which of these?
a. New Brunswick
b. Ontario
c. Vermont
d. Quebec

13. What was the War of Jenkins' Ear (1739–1742)?

a. A war between England and France over borders in New England

b. A war between England and Spain over the colony of Georgia, which remained British

c. A war between England and Spain over the colony of Georgia, which became Spanish for a while

d. A war between Spain and France over the right to trade with the British colonies

14. WHAT ANIMAL DID EUROPEANS BRING TO AMERICA IN THE SEVENTEENTH CENTURY?

Match the Eastern Native American tribes with the approximate area of where they lived before they were forced to leave:

15. Chickasaw   a. Georgia
16. Cherokee   b. Mississippi
17. Choctaw   c. Mississippi
18. Creek   d. Florida
19. Seminole   e. Alabama

20. Which American president sent Lewis and Clark out West to explore, because he wanted American merchants to have greater access the ports of China?

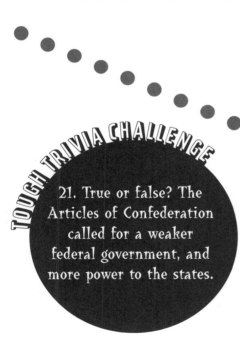

TOUGH TRIVIA CHALLENGE

21. True or false? The Articles of Confederation called for a weaker federal government, and more power to the states.

22. WHAT WAS THE CURRENCY ACT OF 1764?

A. IT CHANGED THE BRITISH MONEY SYSTEM INTO THE ONE USED TODAY.

B. IT CREATED NEW MONEY FOR THE AMERICAN COLONIES.

C. IT REQUIRED COLONISTS TO PAY BRITISH MERCHANTS IN SILVER AND GOLD.

D. IT INSISTED THAT THE COLONISTS USE ONLY PAPER MONEY.

23. How did the American colonies react to the Stamp Act of 1765?

a. They protested and wrote an official response

b. They wanted it expanded to include more about printing and paper, and their response explained why

c. There weren't sure of how it would play out but accepted it for the time being

d. They were relieved that a sense of order was being given over the confusing laws about printing

MATCH THE FOLLOWING NINETEENTH-CENTURY BUSINESSMEN WITH THEIR MAIN INDUSTRIES:

24. John D. Rockefeller

25. J. P. Morgan

26. Andrew Carnegie

27. William Randolph Hearst

28. Cornelius Vanderbilt

a. Business financier

b. Oil

c. Railroad

d. Steel

e. Newspaper

29. What caused the French and Indian War (1754–1763)?

a. An argument between France and Native American tribes over lands in Quebec

b. An argument between British colonists and the French over the right to some lands in Pennsylvania

c. An argument between British colonists and Native Americans over lands, which the French got involved in

d. An argument between Britain and Spain over who had the right to trade with Native American tribes in French colonies

30. Samuel Adams' 1768 Massachusetts Circular Letter said which of these things?

a. Taxes must be negotiated between the colonies and Britain, and that these Acts were a good start

b. That taxation without representation was unconstitutional; he encouraged the colonies to protest the new taxes by boycotting British goods

c. That the British were acting like tyrants and that the American colonies should revolt

d. That the British were trying to compromise on taxes and the colonies should accept this

31. What did the American colonies create in response to the so-called "Intolerable Acts"?

a. The First Confederate Congress
b. The First Continental Congress
c. The First American Parliament
d. The First Continental Monarchy

32. True or false? Eli Whitney's cotton engine (or cotton gin) of 1794 wasn't very important in the history of nineteenth-century America

33. COLONIAL MILITIAS THAT COULD MOBILIZE QUICKLY TO FIGHT THE BRITISH WERE KNOWN AS WHICH OF THESE?

A. QUICK REBELS
B. YANKEES
C. COLONY SOLDIERS
D. MINUTEMEN

Answers: 23. a; 24. b; 25. a; 26. d; 27. e; 28. c; 29. b; 30. b; 31. b; 32. False, it was one of the most impactful inventions of the century; 33. d

History • 9

34. The Declaration of Rights and Sentiments of 1848 wanted equal rights for who?

a. Women   b. Slaves

c. Children   d. Native Americans

MATCH EACH PRESIDENT WITH THEIR POLITICAL PARTY:

35. JOHN ADAMS   A. DEMOCRAT

36. JAMES MADISON   B. WHIG

37. MILLARD FILLMORE   C. REPUBLICAN

38. THEODORE ROOSEVELT   D. DEMOCRATIC-REPUBLICAN

39. JOHN F. KENNEDY   E. FEDERALIST

40. WHO WARNED THAT DEMOCRACY COULD LEAD TO A "TYRANNY OF THE MAJORITY" THAT WOULD HURT MINORITIES AND INDIVIDUALS?

41. In *Dred Scott v. Sandford*, the Supreme Court ruled which of these?

a. That slavery was abolished

b. That Congress did have the authority to stop or limit the spread of slavery into new American territories

c. That Congress did not have the authority to stop or limit the spread of slavery into new American territories

d. That slavery could exist in any state

42. Many late nineteenth-century Americans were unhappy with the government; what did they do about it?

a. They tried to leave the country **b. They planned a revolution**
c. They created new political parties **d. They ignored what was happening**

43. What did President Woodrow Wilson want to create after World War I?

   a. The League of Nations
   b. The United World League
   c. The United Nations
   d. The World Alliance

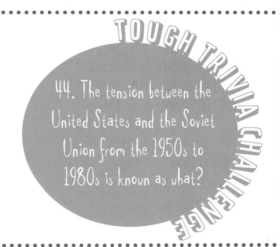

TOUGH TRIVIA CHALLENGE

44. The tension between the United States and the Soviet Union from the 1950s to 1980s is known as what?

Match the American woman with her key contribution to history:

45. Susan B. Anthony a. Computer scientist and Navy Rear Admiral
46. Harriet Tubman b. First woman astronaut to go to space
47. Sacagawea c. Mathematician and "human computer" for NASA
48. Grace Hopper d. Fought for women's right to vote
49. Amelia Earhart e. Abolitionist and women's rights activist
50. Sojourner Truth f. First woman to serve in Congress
51. Sally Ride g. Leading woman of the Civil Rights Movement
52. Rosa Parks h. First woman to fly solo across the Atlantic Ocean
53. Jeannette Rankin i. "Conductor" of the Underground Railroad
54. Dorothy Vaughan j. Lemhi Shoshone woman who guided Lewis and Clark

55. Where was Abraham Lincoln assassinated?

__ __ __ __ __ __

56. In August 1969, what huge music festival took place in New York state?

a. Hippie Fest
b. Woodstock
c. Big Music USA
d. The Summer of Love

57. Which of these was a popular entertainment for urban working class American people in the late nineteenth century?

a. Opera
b. Ballet
c. Vaudeville
d. Museums

TOUGH TRIVIA CHALLENGE

58. President Jimmy Carter negotiated peace between which two countries in 1978?

59. Which city did the British take after the Battle of White Plains in 1776, which helped them control the area?

a. Boston
b. New York
c. Philadelphia
d. Concord

60. The Louisiana Purchase did what for the size of the United States?

a. Added about 25 percent
b. Reduced it for a while
c. Doubled it
d. Tripled it

61. TRUE OR FALSE? MARTIN LUTHER KING JR. ADVOCATED FOR NON-VIOLENT CIVIL DISOBEDIENCE.

62. What did the Thirteenth Amendment of the Constitution guarantee?
- a. The end of slavery in the United States
- b. The right for freed slaves to vote
- c. The right for women to vote
- d. A new definition of treason

63. Which Civil War battle in 1861 was won by the south and meant that the war would continue for a long time?
- a. Shiloh
- b. Bull Run
- c. Gettysburg
- d. Midway

64. The American and French armies won the final victory during the revolutionary war against the British in which battle?
- a. Yorktown
- b. Washington
- c. Camden
- d. Charleston

65. The Erie Canal linked which of these to the Great Lakes?
- a. The Potomac and Washington D.C.
- b. The Charles River and Boston
- c. The Hudson River and New York City
- d. The Ohio River and Louisville, Kentucky

66. What was nullification?
a. The idea that judges could set aside a law they believed was unjust
b. The idea that Congress could override the president and rewrite laws
c. The idea that states could ignore a federal law that they didn't like
d. The idea that banks could tell government to ignore certain laws

◆ ◆ ◆ ◆ ◆ ◆ ◆ ◆ ◆ ◆ ◆ ◆ ◆ ◆ ◆ ◆

67. True or false?
Traditional African rituals, stories, and customs provided a sense of community and identity for southern slaves.

68. What was Prohibition in the 1920s?
a. A constitutional ban on the sale of cigarettes
b. A constitutional ban on the sale of alcohol
c. A federal law against criticizing the government
d. A state law on where one could move and live

◆ ◆ ◆ ◆ ◆ ◆ ◆ ◆ ◆ ◆ ◆ ◆ ◆ ◆ ◆ ◆

69. What was true about music on the radio in the mid-1950s?
a. It was mostly swing and jazz
b. It was mainly classical music for older listeners
c. A lot of it was rock 'n' roll
d. A lot of it was blues music

◆ ◆

70. What was President Theodore Roosevelt's famous motto?
a. Shout and be respected
b. Speak loudly and be heard
c. Never speak but show by your deeds
d. Speak softly and carry a big stick

71. What was it about President Franklin D. Roosevelt that made him appealing to so many Americans?
   a. He was the first African-American president
   b. He came from a poor family and was poor his whole life
   c. He was a president for the "common man"
   d. He was European, but became a U.S. citizen

72. What happened in 1929 that affected the United States and the world?
a. World War I ended   b. The United States almost broke apart again
c. The stock market crashed   d. World War II began

73. The bombing of Pearl Harbor on December 7, 1941 was known as what?
   a. A day which we will always honor
   b. A date which will live in infamy
   c. A date that marks the start of war
   d. A day we will never forget

74. WHAT WAS THE TREATY OF PARIS OF 1783?

   A. BRITAIN RECOGNIZED AMERICAN INDEPENDENCE AND ITS BOUNDARIES

   B. BRITAIN GAVE UP ALL CLAIMS TO ANY LANDS IN THE WESTERN HEMISPHERE

   C. FRANCE RECOGNIZED AMERICAN INDEPENDENCE

   D. FRANCE GAVE CONTROL OF ITS COLONIES TO BRITAIN

75. How did the American Revolution change women's lives?

    a. They gained the right to vote

    b. They had the chance to run for public office

    c. They received equality with men

    d. They gained new opportunities for education

---

76. Which American river was important for transporting cotton in the nineteenth century?

    a. The Rio Grande

    b. The Mississippi River

    c. The Hudson River

    d. The Russian River

77. How was California admitted to the Union?

    a. As a slave state

    b. As a free state

    c. As a state that could choose to be free or have slaves

    d. As both a free (northern) and slave (southern) state

78. Which country could the Confederacy no longer export cotton to, beginning in 1861, because of a Union naval blockade?

    a. Brazil   b. Britain   c. Spain   d. France

79. Who invented the telephone?

a. Eli Whitney

b. Alexander Graham Bell

c. George Washington Carver

d. Isambard Kingdom Brunel

---

80. Why did a lot of people from countries, such as Italy, Greece, and Eastern Europe, come to America in beginning in the 1880s?

    a. They wanted to work for a while, but ended up staying instead

    b. They were pushed out by famine, poverty, and political problems

    c. They wanted to go to England or France, but couldn't

    d. Many were criminals, running from the law

81. What was a main reason that the United States entered World War I?

    a. A chance to take over parts of Europe

    b. Strong economic ties with Great Britain

    c. The new American president wanted to end the war

    d. The army wanted it

82. What was the "Red Scare" that began in 1919?

    a. Fear of factory workers going on strike

    b. Fear of a renewed war in Europe

    c. Fear of Asian countries uniting against the United States

    d. Fear of communist spies trying to overthrow the government

TOUGH TRIVIA CHALLENGE

83. TRUE OR FALSE? ABRAHAM LINCOLN'S POPULARITY ACTUALLY DECREASED DURING THE CIVIL WAR.

84. Who were the muckrakers?

    a. A new political party

    b. Striking factory workers

    c. Journalists who wanted to expose American society's problems

    d. The name of a branch of the United States Army

85. What caused the Depression of 1893?

    a. Too many immigrants couldn't find work

    b. Railroads grew too quickly and ran out of money

    c. Too much government spending

    d. A shortage of gold

86. In 1898, South Dakota was the first state to allow which of the following?

a. A woman to run for governor
b. The people to vote on ballot initiatives
c. Black men to vote
d. Women to vote

87. What did the Texas Consultation delegates do in March of 1836?

a. They pledged loyalty to Mexico in exchange for various rights
b. They declared that they were now a part of the United States
c. They declared independence from Mexico and wrote a new constitution
d. They declared war on Mexico

88. By 1850, which of these cities had grown large, attracting people from China and South America, as a result of the new "gold rush"?

a. Santa Cruz
b. San Francisco
c. Sacramento
d. San Jose

89. Which of the following things is true about Nat Turner's Rebellion in 1831?

a. It wasn't important in the history of abolition and the fight against slavery.
b. It inspired more rebellions and almost ended slavery even before the Civil War.
c. It failed from the beginning.
d. It was one of the biggest slave revolts in American history.

90. Which of these was invented by Robert Fulton in 1807?

a. The first electric light bulb
b. The steam locomotive
c. The telegraph
d. The steamship engine

TOUGH TRIVIA CHALLENGE

91. What did the British forces successfully do in July 1814?

a. They burned New York City to the ground
b. They defeated the Americans in Massachussets
c. They burned Washington, D.C. to the ground
d. They destroyed Boston

92. TRUE OR FALSE? PRESIDENT JOHNSON'S GREAT SOCIETY POLICY OF THE 1960S MAINLY WANTED TO END SEGREGATION.

93. Which of these was a popular character in slave stories, a trickster who outwitted his opponents?
a. The Voodoo Cat
b. The Big Bear
c. The Coyote
d. Brer Rabbit

TOUGH TRIVIA CHALLENGE

95. WHO WAS PRESIDENT DURING THE LAST DAYS OF WORLD WAR II?

94. In 1900, an average American factory worker worked how many hours per week?
a. 50 b. 40
c. 60 d. 30

96. True or false? Farmers were hurt especially badly during the Great Depression.

97. What island did Native American activists occupy in November, 1969?

98. The Treaty of Guadalupe Hidalgo, signed in February 1848, led to which result?
a. Mexico increased its size to include California and Nevada
b. Mexico regained almost all of Texas
c. Mexico gave nearly half its land to the United States
d. Mexico gave Mexico City to the United States

99. The nineteenth-century idea that Americans were chosen to spread across the continent is known as what?

100. The New Deal attempted to help with the problems caused by what?

101. The evil, scheming ruler of England during the Robin Hood stories was:

a. Richard   b. Henry   c. John   d. Stephen

102. True or false? King John of England was actually said to be a nice and reasonable man, well-liked by his barons.

103. Which was true about football in medieval England?

a. It was the most popular game of the time
b. Early football leagues already existed
c. It was dangerous and banned by the 14th century
d. It was the favorite sport of nobles and kings

104. Which of these was one of the stages of learning a trade in a guild?

a. Master   b. Journeyman
c. Apprentice   d. All of the above

105. WHO WAS THE MOST FAMOUS DOMINICAN PHILOSOPHER OF THE MIDDLE AGES?

A. THOMAS MALTHUS
B. THOMAS HANKS
C. THOMAS AQUINAS
D. THOMAS MANN

TOUGH TRIVIA CHALLENGE

106. The medieval organizations where young men would go to learn a specific trade were called:
a. Guilds   b. Workhouses
c. Universities
d. Trade schools

MATCH THE HISTORICAL FIGURES WITH THE BATTLES
THEY ARE MOST FAMOUS FOR FIGHTING IN:

107. Edward III

108. Henry V

109. Saladin

110. William the Conqueror

111. Richard the Lionheart

112. Charles Martel

113. Richard III

114. Harald Hardrada

115. Robert the Bruce

116. Mehmed the Conqueror

a. The Battle of Tours (732 CE)

b. Hattin (1187 CE)

c. Bannockburn (1314 CE)

d. The Third Crusade (1189–1192 CE)

e. The Battle of Crécy (1346 CE)

f. Bosworth Field (1485 CE)

g. Hastings (1066 CE)

h. Battle of Stamford Bridge (1066 CE)

i. The Siege of Constantinople (1453 CE)

j. Agincourt (1415 CE)

117. What was the name of the great Mongol leader of the thirteenth century, whose empire eventually reached across Asia into Eastern Europe?

118. The Albigensian Crusade against perceived heretics took place in which region?
   a. Northern France
   b. Southern England
   c. Southern France
   d. Western Germany

119. Where were castles usually built?
   a. By rivers
   b. In valleys
   c. In forests
   d. On hilltops

Answers: 101. c; 102. False; he was so unpopular with the barons that they rebelled against him, leading to the First Barons' War; 103. c; 104. d; 105. c; 106. a; 107. e; 108. j; 109. b; 110. g; 111. d; 112. a; 113. f; 114. h; 115. c; 116. i; 117. Genghis Khan; 118. c; 119. d

History • 21

120. Someone who farmed the land owned by a noble and was obligated to give him a portion of their crops was called what?
a. An indentured servant
b. A sharecropper
c. A serf
d. A slave

▲▲▲▲▲▲▲▲▲▲▲▲▲▲

121. The Vikings came mainly from which area?
a. Norway
b. Sweden
c. Denmark
d. All of the above

122. Which game did the Moors introduce in Spain, that became popular in the rest of Europe?
a. Archery   b. Charades
c. Football   d. Chess

123. What was true about medieval animals?
a. Otters and beavers were considered to be fish
b. Animals could be put on trial for committing crimes
c. Farm animals were often smaller than their modern versions
d. All of the above

▲▲▲▲▲▲▲▲▲▲▲▲▲▲▲▲▲▲▲▲▲▲▲▲▲▲

MATCH EACH MONARCH WITH THE COUNTRY OR REGION THAT THEY RULED OR CONTROLLED:

124. Henry II	a. Ireland
125. Saladin	b. France
126. Robert the Bruce	c. Scotland
127. Harald Bluetooth	d. England and Western France
128. Richard II	e. Denmark and Norway
129. Osman I	f. Turkey
130. Louis IX	g. Germany and Italy
131. Alphonso X	h. Castile (Spain)
132. Frederick II	i. The Holy Land
133. Brian Boru	j. England

134. Which was true of students and Oxford and Paris Universities?

a. They had a much easier course of study than modern students

b. They were made up of both men and women

c. They had all of their expenses paid for by their governments

d. They often clashed with the locals, who resented them

▲ ▲ ▲ ▲ ▲ ▲ ▲ ▲ ▲ ▲ ▲ ▲ ▲ ▲

135. True or false? When the Mongols invaded Europe from the East, they were easily defeated by the Hungarians and other countries that united to stop them.

▲ ▲ ▲ ▲ ▲ ▲ ▲ ▲ ▲ ▲ ▲ ▲ ▲ ▲

136. Which of the following was invented during the Middle Ages?

a. The horse saddle
b. Armor
c. The clock
d. Soap

▲ ▲ ▲ ▲ ▲ ▲ ▲ ▲ ▲ ▲ ▲ ▲ ▲ ▲

137. TRUE OR FALSE? JOUSTING TOURNAMENTS WERE VERY DANGEROUS AND SOMETIMES JOUSTERS WERE ACCIDENTALLY INJURED OR KILLED.

TOUGH TRIVIA CHALLENGE

138. What Old English poem tells the story of a hero who fights the monster Grendel?

139. The old Roman Empire split into two parts, ruled from which cities?

a. Rome and Jerusalem
b. Paris and Constantinople
c. Rome and Constantinople
d. Aachen and Antioch

▲ ▲ ▲ ▲ ▲ ▲ ▲ ▲ ▲ ▲ ▲ ▲ ▲ ▲

140. Which mathematical system did the Arabs introduce during the Middle Ages?

a. Long division   b. Algebra
c. Calculus   d. Geometry

TOUGH TRIVIA CHALLENGE

141. True or false? At various times, the Anglo-Saxons elected their kings.

143. WHO DEFEATED THE ENGLISH AT HASTINGS IN SOUTH ENGLAND IN 1066?

142. Beginning in the fourteenth century, Europe was hit by a change in climate later known as:
a. **The Little Ice Age**
b. **The Great Warming**
c. **The Great Ice Age**
d. **The Terrible Warming**

144. TRUE OR FALSE? EVERYONE BELIEVED THAT THE WORLD WAS FLAT UNTIL COLUMBUS SAILED IN 1492 AND PROVED IT WASN'T.

MATCH THE MEDIEVAL PROFESSION WITH ITS NAME:

145. Chandler
146. Apothecary
147. Luthier
148. Catchpole
149. Marshal
150. Stationer
151. Hayward
152. Carder
153. Woodward
154. Thonger

a. Maker and seller of medicines
b. Seller of books and sometimes a scribe
c. Tender of hedges and keeper of fences on an estate
d. Candle maker
e. Maker of leather straps and laces
f. Comber of wool in preparation for spinning
g. Builder of stringed instruments
h. Tender of the horses of a lord
i. Keeper of a forest
j. Debt and tax finder and collector

155. Marco Polo was famous for traveling as far as which country in the thirteenth century?

156. In practice, what needed to happen for an average medieval couple to marry?
   a. They had to have the wedding performed by a priest
   b. They had to declare that they wanted to marry each other
   c. They had to obtain their parents' permission
   d. They had to do so in a church

157. What was a trencher?
   a. Someone who dug ditches for a living
   b. A soldier who was serving in the trenches
   c. A piece of day-old bread used as a plate
   d. Someone who cleaned the royal stables

158. True or false? William Wallace was a Scottish nobleman who led a revolt against the English and King Edward I in the late thirteenth century.

159. True or false? The Black Death (bubonic plague) killed about 75% of Europe's population in the 14th century.

160. Who was the "Maid of Orleans"?
   a. Margery Kemp
   b. Joan of Arc
   c. Joan the Mad
   d. Lady Jane Grey

161. The man who oversaw a medieval English town or village was called a "Shire-reeve," which gave us which modern word?

162. Which group ruled parts of medieval Spain for seven centuries?
   a. The Blue Men   b. The Berbers
   c. The Bedouins   d. The Moors

Answers: 141. True; 142. a; 143. William the Conqueror; 144. False, the fact that the world was a sphere was well known at the time; 145. d; 146. a; 147. g; 148. j; 149. h; 150. b; 151. c; 152. f; 153. i; 154. e; 155. China; 156. b; 157. c; 158. True; 159. False, the Black Death killed between 30 to 50% of the population of Europe at the time; 160. b; 161. Sheriff; 162. d

163. The Anglo-Saxon king who fought off the Vikings and effectively "saved" England in the 9th century was which of the following?

    a. Alfred the Great
    b. Athelstan the Brave
    c. Albert the Great
    d. Alfred the Mighty

164. Who was crowned emperor on Christmas day in the year 800?

    a. Alfred
    b. William the Conqueror
    c. Charlemagne
    d. Arthur

165. True or false? Women could not own property in the Middle Ages.

166. The ditch around a castle filled with water was used as a defense; what was it called?

    a. Mere
    b. Moat
    c. Mire
    d. Motte

167. Which of the following was a famous and powerful order of fighting monks?

    a. The Knights Templar
    b. The Knights Hospitaller
    c. The Teutonic Knights
    d. All of the above

168. Which two famous monarchs defeated the Moors in Granada in 1492, expelling them from Spain forever?

169. The sons of King Edward IV (who died in 1483) were better known as what?

    a. The Boys Who Lived
    b. The Princes Left Alone
    c. The Orphans of the King
    d. The Princes in the Tower

170. Who was the author of the famous *Canterbury Tales*?

a. Geoffrey of Monmouth
b. Geoffrey Chaucer
c. William Shakespeare
d. They were anonymous

171. Which was founded first, the University of Oxford, or the University of Cambridge?

172. TRUE OR FALSE? IN THE FOURTEENTH CENTURY, THERE WERE TWO POPES, ONE IN ROME AND ONE IN AVIGNON (FRANCE).

173. What secret group of individuals terrorized the medieval Middle East?

a. The Frighteners
b. The Brotherhood
c. The Assassins
d. The Secret Seven

174. The priest who famously clashed with King Henry II of England in the twelfth century and was later murdered was which of the following?

a. Anselm of Canterbury
b. Bede
c. Thomas Becket
d. Thomas Aquinas

TOUGH TRIVIA CHALLENGE

175. Which of the following was a luxury ingredient in food served at the wealthy medieval dinner table?

a. Cinnamon
b. Black pepper
c. Cloves
d. All of the above

176. The document that King John was forced to sign in 1215 was called what?

a. The Macro Carta
b. The Laws of the Barons
c. His own abdication of the throne
d. The Magna Carta

177. The stories of how the Vikings sailed to Iceland and Greenland and colonized them are known as what?
a. Sonnets b. Sagas
c. Epics   d. Adventures

178. According to medieval legend, there was once a woman pope; what was her name?
a. Joan
b. Jane
c. Jean
d. Jan

179. A teenaged boy training to be a knight was known as what?
a. An apprentice   b. A squire
c. A serf   d. A journeyman

180. Mead, a popular Viking drink, was an alcoholic drink made mainly with what?
a. Sugar
b. Berries
c. Apples
d. Honey

181. The medieval singer-poets of southern France were called what?
a. The goliards
b. The trouvères
c. The troubadours
d. The minnesingers

182. WHAT WAS THE OUTCOME OF THE FIRST CRUSADE IN 1099?

183. What style of church architecture came after the Romanesque style?

a. Neo-Classical

b. Gothic

c. Perpendicular

d. Baroque

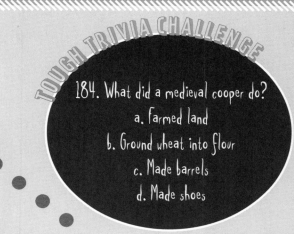

TOUGH TRIVIA CHALLENGE

184. What did a medieval cooper do?

a. Farmed land

b. Ground wheat into flour

c. Made barrels

d. Made shoes

185. What was a secretary to an important medieval noble or monarch called?

a. A professor   b. A scribe   c. A master of writing   d. A chancellor

186. The practice of coloring and decorating manuscripts is known as:

a. Elaboration   b. Illumination

c. Coloration   d. Decoration

187. True or false? Up until 1400, people were often burned at the stake for being witches.

188. What was the family name of the infamous fifteenth-century cruel prince of Wallachia in southern Romania, known for impaling his victims on wooden stakes?

Answers: 177: b; 178: a; 179: b; 180: d; 181: c; 182: It succeeded in capturing Jerusalem for the European armies; 183: b; 184: c; 185: d; 186: b; 187: False, the burning of "heretics" at the stake did not end until the 1600s; 188: Dracula

History • 29

189. What was the name of the group of penitential people who wandered and beat themselves with whips to atone for their sins?

  a. The flagellants
  b. The Whipping Boys
  c. The Sinners
  d. The Atoners

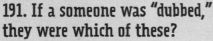

190. What did King Edward I of England famously build in Wales?

191. If a someone was "dubbed," they were which of these?

  a. Knighted
  b. Arrested
  c. Executed
  d. Confirmed

192. Which semi-mythical king inspired dozens of medieval tales of chivalry and great deeds?

  a. Cole
  b. Lear
  c. Arthur
  d. Macbeth

193. Dominicans and Franciscans were special kinds of monks known as what?
  a. Hermits
  b. Friars
  c. Cloistered monks
  d. Priests

TOUGH TRIVIA CHALLENGE

194. Who was King Henry II's famous and remarkable wife?
  a. Blanche of Castile
  b. Eleanor of Aquitaine
  c. Marian of Nottingham
  d. Mary Queen of Scots

195. What weapon gave English armies an advantage in battles of the later Middle Ages?

  a. The crossbow
  b. The longbow
  c. The longsword
  d. The catapult

196. What is the name of the trickster fox in medieval French literature who always gets the better of others?

      a. Reynold   b. Reynard

      c. Richard   d. Rollo

197. The system of owing allegiance and service to a lord or king in exchange for protection and rewards was known as what?

      a. Chivalry   b. Martialism

      c. Feudalism   d. Courtesy

198. The place where monks lived was called which of these?

      a. An abbey   b. A monastery

      c. A priory   d. All of the above

199. St. Francis was said to have preached to who?

      a. The ocean   b. The animals

      c. The trees   d. The deaf

200. WHERE DID THE VIKINGS SAIL TO AROUND THE YEAR 1000?

      A. CHINA   B. NORTH AMERICA

      C. AUSTRALIA   D. INDIA

Answers: 189. a; 190. Five castles (or just "castles"); 191. a; 192. c; 193. b; 194. b; 195. b; 196. b; 197. c; 198. d; 199. b; 200. b

CHAPTER 2

Culture & Entertainment

DC COMICS

201. What does the symbol on Superman's chest mean?

   a. Strength   b. Hope   c. Peace   d. Justice

202. What is Barbara Gordon's (Batgirl, Oracle) relationship to Police Commissioner Jim Gordon?

   a. Sister   b. Wife   c. Daughter   d. Cousin

203. What is the Penguin's real name?

   a. Oderic Copperpot   b. Oswald Cobblepot
   c. Ozric Crockpot   d. Orville Crackpot

MATCH EACH DC COMICS CHARACTER WITH THE TEAM THEY ARE MOST OFTEN ASSOCIATED WITH:

204. Zatanna   a. Suicide Squad

205. Captain Boomerang   b. Legion of Superheroes

206. Lex Luthor   c. League of Assassins

207. Superman   d. Justice League Dark

208. Ra's al Ghul   e. Doom Patrol

209. Starfire   f. Green Lantern Corps

210. Saturn Girl   g. Teen Titans (or Titans)

211. Kilowog   h. Injustice League

212. Huntress   i. Birds of Prey

213. Robotman   j. Justice League

214. J'onn J'onzz was born on which planet?

215. True or false? **The Joker's past is whatever he says it is at any given time; no one even knows his real name.**

216. Which Greek god is Wonder Woman's main enemy?
   a. Hades
   b. Ares
   c. Zeus
   d. Hermes

217. A Mother Box creates interstellar pathways over huge distances. These paths have a nickname, what is it?
   a. Wormholes
   b. Space Dividers
   c. Boom Tubes
   d. Galactic Tunnels

218. Shazam has also gone by which other name?
   a. Captain Wonder
   b. Captain Magnificnet
   c. Captain Marvel
   d. Captain Freedom

219. In the 1940s, DC sued Fawcett Publications, claiming that their hero Captain Marvel was too similar to which DC character?
   a. Batman
   b. Green Lantern
   c. Superman
   d. The Flash

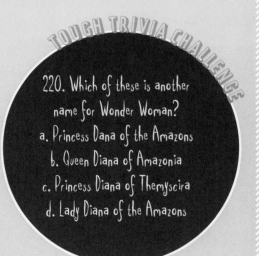

TOUGH TRIVIA CHALLENGE

220. Which of these is another name for Wonder Woman?
   a. Princess Dana of the Amazons
   b. Queen Diana of Amazonia
   c. Princess Diana of Themyscira
   d. Lady Diana of the Amazons

221. Why is Superman so powerful on Earth?

a. Because of the light and energy of our sun
b. Because of the nature of our atmosphere
c. Because of special energy from the Fortress of Solitude
d. Because of his suit

222. TRUE OR FALSE?
BATMAN (BRUCE WAYNE) AND CATWOMAN (SELINA KYLE) CALLED OFF THEIR WEDDING AT THE LAST MINUTE.

223. True or false? Lex Luthor knows that Clark Kent is Superman.

224. What is DA Harvey Dent famous for?

a. Defending Bruce Wayne against false charges
b. Becoming the hero called Gotham
c. Prosecuting the Joker for his crimes
d. Becoming the villain Two-Face after an accident

MATCH EACH DC CHARACTER OR HERO WITH THE ROMANTIC PARTNER OR SPOUSE THEY ARE MOST OFTEN ASSOCIATED WITH:

225. Barry Allen (The Flash)
226. Oliver Queen (Green Arrow)
227. Raven
228. Scott Free (Mr. Miracle)
229. Pamela Isley (Poison Ivy)
230. Sue Dibny
231. Wonder Woman
232. Midnighter
233. Clark Kent (Superman)
234. Aquaman

a. Big Barda
b. Lois Lane
c. The Elongated Man
d. Iris West
e. Black Canary
f. Apollo
g. Mera
h. Beast Boy
i. Harley Quinn
j. Steve Trevor

235. WHICH TWO MAJOR HEROES DIED DURING *CRISIS ON INFINITE EARTHS?*

236. Which secret, government-sponsored group does Amanda Waller direct?

a. The Forgotten Heroes
b. The Suicide Squad
c. The Secret Six
d. The Injustice League

237. The teenager Billy Batson becomes which powerful superhero?

a. Kid Flash
b. Dr. Fate
c. A Green Lantern
d. Shazam

238. Before she became Batwoman, Kate Kane did what?

a. Was a mercenary
b. Served in the Army
c. Was an Air Force pilot
d. Served in the Navy

239. True or false? Wally West has been both Kid Flash and the Flash.

240. The two female superheroes from Earth 2 trying to get back there from the main earth in the recent *World's Finest* comic series were who?

a. Supergirl and Saturn Girl
b. Huntress and Black Canary
c. Supergirl and Power Girl
d. Huntress and Power Girl

241. What was Wonder Woman's original name going to be, before it was changed?

a. Amazonia
b. Suprema
c. Antiope
d. Athena

242. True or false? **The Watchmen, by Lana Moore, was originally going to include some classic DC comics characters.**

243. Harley Quinn, Poison Ivy, and Catwoman starred in their own comic book series named what?

244. **In the new Justice League, after *Crisis on Infinite Earths*, who of the following was a founding member?**
   a. Batman
   b. Mr. Miracle
   c. Dr. Fate
   d. All of the above

245. Which of these was something Superman could not do when he was first created?
   a. Have super strength
   b. Fly
   c. Stop bullets
   d. Jump over buildings

246. **Which emotion drives the Red Lanterns?**
   a. Rage
   b. Fear
   c. Embarrassment
   d. Sadness

247. Oracle and Black Canary were the core members of which superhero team?
   a. Hawk and Dove
   b. Secret Six
   c. Birds of Prey
   d. The Movement

248. In her most famous version, Supergirl (Kara Zor-El) has what relation to Superman?
   a. His wife
   b. His cousin
   c. His sister
   d. His aunt

Answers: 235. Supergirl and The Flash; 236. b; 237. d; 238. b; 239. True; 240. d; 241. b; 242. True; 243. Gotham City Sirens; 244. d; 245. b; 246. a; 247. c; 248. b.

Culture & Entertainment • **37**

249. The Green Lantern Simon Baz was controversial with other heroes (especially Batman) because he carried what?
   a. Tear gas   b. A sword   c. A knife   d. A gun

▲▲▲▲▲▲▲▲▲▲▲▲▲▲▲▲▲▲▲▲▲▲

250. Blue Beetle (Ted Kord) has often teamed up with which hero from the future?
   a. Booster Gold   b. Mon-El
   c. Lightning Lad   d. Dragonwing

251. With whom has Kate Kane (Batwoman) been linked romantically?
   a. Maggie Sawyer   b. Renee Montoya
   c. Safiyah Sohail   d. All of the above

252. Superman's x-ray vision works on every material except which of these?
   a. Copper   b. Lead   c. Gold   d. Iron

▲▲▲▲▲▲▲▲▲▲▲▲▲▲▲▲▲▲▲▲▲▲

253. THE WOMEN OF PRINCESS DIANA'S (WONDER WOMAN'S) HOMELAND ARE KNOWN AS:
   A. SIRENS   B. GODDESSES
   C. OLYMPIANS   D. AMAZONS

▲▲▲▲▲▲▲▲▲▲▲▲▲▲▲▲▲▲▲▲▲▲

254. TRUE OR FALSE? ARTEMIS TOOK ON THE TITLE OF "WONDER WOMAN" FOR A SHORT TIME.

MATCH THE FOLLOWING DC CHARACTERS WITH THEIR POWERS:

255. Brainiac
256. Superman
257. Aquaman
258. Batman
259. Martian Manhunter
260. The Flash
261. John Constantine
262. Green Lantern
263. Vixen
264. Poison Ivy

a. Nearly unlimited intelligence and knowledge
b. Controls water, communicates with fish
c. Powerful warlock and magic user
d. Controls and manipulates plants
e. Uses the powers of animal spirits
f. Telepath and shape-shifter
g. Flight, strength, x-ray vision
h. Super speed
i. Uses a cosmic ring to manipulate reality
j. No non-natural powers

▲▲▲▲▲▲▲▲▲▲▲▲▲▲▲▲▲▲▲▲▲▲▲▲▲▲▲▲▲▲

265. WHAT IS THE TWIN PLANET OF APOKOLIPS?

▲▲▲▲▲▲▲▲▲▲▲▲▲▲▲▲▲▲▲▲▲▲▲▲▲▲▲▲▲▲

266. Batman was created by:

a. Jerry Siegel and Jack Kirby
b. Bob Kane and Bill Finger
c. Jack Kirby and Stan Lee
d. Bob Kane and Stan Lee

267. Zinda Blake comes from the past and has worked with the Birds of Prey under which name?

a. Lady Darkwing
b. Madame Raptor
c. Lady Blackhawk
d. Ms. Nighthawk

Answers: 249. d; 250. a; 251. d; 252. b; 253. d; 254. True; 255. a; 256. g; 257. b; 258. j; 259. f; 260. h; 261. c; 262. i; 263. e; 264. d; 265. New Genesis; 266. b; 267. c.

Culture & Entertainment • 39

268. Which was the first title where Superman appeared?
a. *Timely Comics*
b. *Action Comics*
c. *Detective Comics*
d. *Sensation Comics*

◆ ◆ ◆ ◆ ◆ ◆ ◆ ◆ ◆

269. What is the Riddler's real name
a. Edward Nygma
b. Eddie Rider
c. Edmund Nygma
d. Edward Ringo

270. The recent *Doomsday Clock* series brings the characters from which other comic book series into the DC Universe?
a. *Infinite Crisis*   b. *Secret Wars*
c. *Secret Invasion*   d. *Watchmen*

271. THE ALIEN PRINCESS KORIAND'R GOES BY WHAT NAME ON EARTH?

272. True or false? When the Joker was first introduced, he was only supposed to be used twice and then never again.

◆ ◆ ◆ ◆ ◆ ◆ ◆ ◆ ◆

273. What is the prison for Gotham's criminally insane called?
a. Arkham Prison   b. Bedlam Penitentiary
c. The Ark   d. Arkham Asylum

◆ ◆ ◆ ◆ ◆ ◆ ◆ ◆ ◆

274. What comic series based in an alternate universe came from a set of statues of female DC superheroes in 1940s-style costumes?
a. *DC Bombshells*
b. *DC War Sirens*
c. *DC Lady Liberators*
d. *DC Daughters of Freedom*

◆ ◆ ◆ ◆ ◆ ◆ ◆ ◆ ◆

275. THE JOKER KILLED WHICH VERSION OF ROBIN?
A. DICK GRAYSON   B. TIM DRAKE
C. JASON TODD   D. CARRIE KELLEY

◆ ◆ ◆ ◆ ◆ ◆ ◆ ◆ ◆

276. True or false? Swamp Thing has mostly been a villain over the years.

277. After the events of *Crisis on Infinite Earths*, what happened?
   a. Only five DC universes were left, all the others were gone
   b. A single DC universe emerged
   c. Multiple new DC universes were created
   d. A hundred DC universes merged into one

TOUGH TRIVIA CHALLENGE

278. Who was the first Flash?
   a. Barry Allen
   b. Jay Garrick
   c. Wally West
   d. Bart Allen

279. Jessica Cruz has assumed the role of which superhero?
   a. Vixen   b. Green Lantern
   c. Hawkgirl   d. Catwoman

280. The name "Shazam" is made up of the first letters of six "immortals." Who are they?

281. Which bounty hunter character refers to himself as "the Main Man"?
   a. Guy Gardner
   b. Catman
   c. Lobo
   d. Deathstroke

282. Who is Wonder Woman's mother?
   a. Queen Artemis
   b. Queen Hippolyta
   c. Queen Persephone
   d. Queen Hera

283. TRUE OR FALSE? BRUCE WAYNE WAS *NOT* THE ORIGINAL BATMAN.

Answers: 268. b; 269. a; 270. d; 271. Starfire; 272. True; 273. d; 274. a; 275. c; 276. False; Swamp Thing is a hero that fights to protect both humanity and the environment; 277. b; 278. b; 279. b; 280. Solomon, Hercules, Atlas, Zeus, Achilles, and Mercury; 281. c; 282. b; 283. False

284. Jean-Paul Valley is the anti-hero Azrael. What other name did he adopt for a short time?

285. How does Zatanna work her magic?
a. She has a magic amulet
b. She uses a wand given to her by her father
c. She speaks the words to her spells backwards
d. She goes into a trance

286. Superman's adoptive mother is Martha Kent. Who is his real mother?
a. Kara Zor-El
b. Lora Kal-El
c. Lara Lor-Van
d. Lana Zor-El

287. Before she became Oracle, Barbara Gordon was which superhero?
a. Black Canary   b. Batgirl
c. Huntress   d. Batwoman

288. CASSANDRA CAIN GOES BY THE NAME ORPHAN IN THE CURRENT DC COMICS RUN. WHAT WAS HER PREVIOUS IDENTITY?

289. Who is Batwoman's secret identity?
a. Kathy Keene
b. Catherine Keel
c. Kate Kane
d. Katie Kenealy

290. For a time, police detective Renee Montoya took on the role of which costumed hero?
a. Huntress   b. The Question
c. Batgirl   d. The Answer

291. How does the villain Bane gain his immense strength?
a. From exposure to Kryptonite
b. From an experimental drug that he must take daily
c. From sunlight; his skin absorbs higher levels of energy
d. From a magic potion prepared by a sorcerer

292. What is another of Batman's titles?
a. The World's Greatest Detective
b. The World's Strongest Human
c. The World's Smartest Hero
d. The World's Darkest Knight

293. WHO HAS APPEARED IN MORE COMICS, BATMAN OR SUPERMAN?

294. What can force Mister Mxyzptlk to go back to his own dimension?

295. True or false? Wonder Woman's creator, William Moulton Marston, created an early version of the lie detector.

296. What did Doomsday do?
a. He defeated the Justice League
b. He killed Superman
c. He destroyed Krypton
d. He became the new Superman

TOUGH TRIVIA CHALLENGE

297. True or false? Jason Todd was the first to adopt the name Robin as Batman's sidekick.

298. Who of the following is a Green Lantern?
a. Guy Gardner
b. Hal Jordan
c. John Stewart
d. All of the above

299. Batman appears in *Detective Comics*, Superman appears in *Action Comics*. What comic did Wonder Woman used to also appear in?
a. *Star Comics*
b. *Sensation Comics*
c. *Superb Comics*
d. *Spectacular Comics*

300. Bruce Wayne's parents were murdered by which criminal?
a. The Red Hood
b. Black Mask
c. Joe Chill
d. Mr. Freeze

Answers: 284. Batman; 285. c; 286. c; 287. b; 288. Batgirl; 289. c; 290. b; 291. b; 292. a; 293. Batman; 294. Getting him to say or spell his name backwards; 295. True; 296. b; 297. False, Dick Grayson appeared as the first Robin in 1940; 298. d; 299. b; 300. c.

MARVEL COMICS

301. She-Hulk's alternate identity, Jennifer Walters, has what job?

a. Doctor   b. Scientist   c. Lawyer   d. Athlete

302. America Chavez (Miss America) comes from what different dimension?

a. The Negative Zone   b. The Utopian Parallel
c. The Dark Dimension   d. The World Tree

303. What is the Silver Surfer's real name?

a. Warren Radd   b. Orin Badd
c. Norrin Radd   d. Loren Sadd

304. What superhero duo first appeared in a Spider-Man comic, using the powers of darkness and light?

305. True or false? Felicia Hardy was bitten by a mutant panther, and gained its powers, calling herself the Black Cat.

306. By the early 1960s, Marvel Comics had emerged out of which earlier comic book company?

a. DC Comics
b. Timely Comics
c. Atlas Comics
d. Entertaining Comics

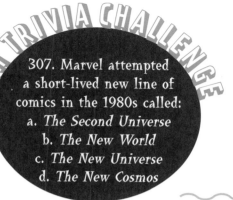

TOUGH TRIVIA CHALLENGE

307. Marvel attempted a short-lived new line of comics in the 1980s called:
a. *The Second Universe*
b. *The New World*
c. *The New Universe*
d. *The New Cosmos*

309. Bucky Barnes, Captain America's friend during World War II, became which villain for several decades?
a. **The Immortal Soldier**
b. **The Autumn Soldier**
c. **The Ice Cream Soldier**
d. **The Winter Soldier**

308. An all-women version of the Defenders formed under what name?
a. The Undefeated Defenders
b. The Mighty Defenders
c. The Amazing Defenders
d. The Fearless Defenders

310. TRUE OR FALSE? CAROL DANVERS, WHO IS CAPTAIN MARVEL, WAS EARLIER KNOWN AS MS. MARVEL.

MATCH THE FOLLOWING MARVEL SUPERHEROES WITH THE TEAMS THEY ARE MOST OFTEN A PART OF:

311. Storm	a. Alpha Flight
312. Iron Man	b. The Defenders
313. Valkyrie	c. The X-Men
314. Rocket Raccoon	d. The Runaways
315. Northstar	e. Guardians of the Galaxy
316. Johnny Storm	f. The Avengers
317. Medusa	g. The Fantastic Four
318. Molly Hayes	h. Daughters of the Dragon
319. Misty Knight	i. Mercs for Money
320. Deadpool	j. The Inhumans

321. What evil organization is a major enemy of S.H.I.E.L.D. and Marvel superheroes in general?

a. SWORD   b. HYDRA   c. SPEAR   d. MEDUSA

TOUGH TRIVIA CHALLENGE

322. Sasquatch has long been a member of which superhero team?
a. The Champions
b. The X-Men
c. Alpha Flight
d. Power Pack

323. Teenage genius Riri Williams followed in the footsteps of what other genius when becoming the hero Iron Heart?
a. Helen Cho
b. Tony Stark
c. Bruce Banner
d. Reed Richards

324. Mutant Jean Grey has hosted in her body which powerful cosmic force?

a. The X-Force   b. The Strong Force
c. The Phoenix Force   d. The A-Force

325. What major problem did Marvel have in the mid-1990s?

a. It was bought by DC
b. It had to file for bankruptcy protection
c. Its writers went on strike
d. Stan Lee quit the company

326. TRUE OR FALSE? A-FORCE WAS AN AVENGERS TEAM MADE UP ENTIRELY OF FEMALE SUPERHEROES.

MATCH EACH MARVEL CHARACTER/HERO WITH THE ROMANTIC PARTNER OR SPOUSE THEY ARE MOST OFTEN ASSOCIATED WITH:

327. Mary Jane Watson
328. Karolina Dean
329. Hulkling
330. Jessica Jones
331. Rogue
332. Betty Ross
333. Sue Storm (The Invisible Woman)
334. Wanda Maximoff (Scarlet Witch)
335. Angela
336. Pepper Pots

a. Tony Stark (Iron Man)
b. Reed Richards (Mr. Fantastic)
c. Luke Cage
d. Peter Parker (Spider-Man)
e. Bruce Banner (the Hulk)
f. Wiccan
g. The Vision
h. Nico Minoru
i. Gambit
j. Sera

---

337. WHO IS THE SECOND HERO TO BE NAMED HAWKEYE, WHO WAS TRAINED BY THE ORIGINAL HAWKEYE, CLINT BARTON?

---

338. Thor's enemy, Malekith the Accursed, rules which group?
a. The Dark Elves
b. The Fire Giants
c. The Dark Trolls
d. The Frost Giants

339. How did Dr. Curtis Conner accidentally become the villain known as the Lizard?
a. He was trying to cure his son's rare illness
b. He was looking for a way to regrow his lost arm
c. He was bitten by a genetically-modified iguana
d. He was accidentally fused with a gecko while teleporting

340. Artist Jack Kirby co-created which of the following?
    a. The Fantastic Four   b. The Avengers
    c. The X-Men   d. All of the above

341. True or false? The Eternals created the Celestials and the Deviants.

342. NICK FURY MOST OFTEN APPEARS AS THE HEAD OF WHICH ORGANIZATION?

343. The symbiote known as Venom most famously bonded with which human?
    a. Eddie Brock   b. Don Blake   c. Ned Leeds   d. Rick Jones

344. Who of these was the identity of the most well-known version of the Spider-Man villain, the Green Goblin?
    a. Norman Osborn
    b. Wilson Fisk
    c. Frank Castle
    d. Adrian Toomes

345. Which of the following heroes was a founding member of the X-Men?
    a. Storm
    b. Psylocke
    c. Angel
    d. Nightcrawler

346. Excalibur was first led by which superhero?
a. Charles Xavier   b. The Black Knight   c. Captain Britain   d. Shadow Cat

347. Daredevil is also known as which of the following?

a. The Man without Faith   **b. The Man without Sight**

c. The Man without Fear   **d. The Man without Limits**

348. How did Silk (Cindy Moon) gain her powers?

a. Bitten by a radioactive silk worm

b. Exposed to radioactive silk clothing

c. Bitten by a radioactive spider

d. She has no special powers

TOUGH TRIVIA CHALLENGE

349. The Vision's synthetic daughter is known as:
a. Synthia
b. Visette
c. Viv
d. Wanda

350. What is unique about Misty Knight?

a. She has a bionic eye that allows her to see far better.

b. She has bionic legs that let her run faster and jump higher.

c. She has bionic hearing that lets her detect the slightest sound.

d. She has a bionic right arm that gives her great strength.

351. TRUE OR FALSE? BEN PARKER IS PETER PARKER'S (SPIDER-MAN'S) FATHER.

352. What is the superhero name of high school student Kamala Khan?

353. What is the name of Jessica Jones' private investigation business?
   a. Undercover Investigations
   b. Alias Investigations
   c. Ethical Investigations
   d. Anonymous Investigations

◆ ◆ ◆ ◆ ◆ ◆ ◆ ◆ ◆ ◆ ◆ ◆ ◆ ◆

354. In 1992, seven of Marvel's top artists left to form which new company?
   a. Vertigo Comics
   b. Image Comics
   c. Darkhorse Comics
   d. Eclipse Comics

◆ ◆ ◆ ◆ ◆ ◆ ◆ ◆ ◆ ◆ ◆ ◆ ◆ ◆

355. What did Marvel stop doing in 2001?
   a. It stopped selling off the rights to its characters to film studios
   b. It stopped submitting its comics to the Comics Code Authority for approval
   c. It stopped accepting unsolicited submissions from artists and writers
   d. It stopped publishing for six months, to reorder the business

◆ ◆ ◆ ◆ ◆ ◆ ◆ ◆ ◆ ◆ ◆ ◆ ◆ ◆

356. True or false?
Mockingbird founded the West Coast Avengers.

◆ ◆

MATCH THE FOLLOWING MARVEL CHARACTERS WITH THEIR POWERS:

357. Professor Charles Xavier
358. Mystique
359. Ant Man
360. Deadpool
361. Ms. Marvel (Kamala Khan)
362. Kitty Pryde
363. Colossus
364. America Chavez
365. Domino
366. Rogue

a. Can transform body into organic steel
b. Is a shape-shifter
c. Has a fast and very powerful healing ability
d. Can temporarily steal another's powers by touching them
e. Can walk through walls and other solid objects
f. Is a powerful telepath
g. Uses a suit to shrink, even down to subatomic levels
h. Can bend luck to their favor
i. Can change the shape and size of body, arms, and legs
j. Can punch star-shaped holes into other dimensions

367. Crime boss Wilson Fisk is better known as:
a. The Chairman   b. The Godfather
c. The Main Man   d. The Kingpin

368. What happened to the original Defenders team?

a. They were betrayed by one of their own

b. They were forced to break up to save the world

c. They argued and refused to work together again

d. They went into another dimension and were lost for years

369. Carol Danvers, the real-life name of Captain Marvel, joined which branch of the armed forces as a young woman?
a. Army   b. Navy
c. Air Force   d. Marines

370. The mutant Emma Frost is also known as:
a. The Black Queen
b. The White Knight
c. The White Queen
d. The Black Bishop

371. Skilled fighter and Guardians of the Galaxy member Gamora was adopted as a child by which powerful cosmic villain?
a. Galactus
b. Thanos
c. Ronan the Accuser
d. The Super Skrull

372. Black Widow originally was trained to be which of these?
a. A British agent   b. An American agent
c. A German agent   d. A Russian agent

Answers: 353. b; 354. b; 355. b; 356. False, the West Coast Avengers were founded by Hawkeye; 357. f; 358. b; 359. g; 360. c; 361. i; 362. e; 363. a; 364. j; 365. h; 366. d; 367. d; 368. b; 369. c; 370. c; 371. b; 372. d.

TOUGH TRIVIA CHALLENGE

373. TRUE OR FALSE? ROGUE WAS A VILLAIN BEFORE SHE JOINED THE X-MEN.

374. Why did Peter Parker decide to use his new Spider-Man abilities to become a hero?

   a. He forgot to take his Aunt May to see a doctor while he was out playing with his powers

   b. He failed to stop a thief who later murdered his Uncle Ben

   c. He ignored fire engines racing to a burning building and people died

   d. He accidentally injured an opponent in a wrestling ring

375. Who first created the Inhumans thousands of years ago?

   a. The Chitauri

   b. The Skrulls

   c. The Watchers

   d. The Kree

376. True or false? The Beyonder was revealed to be another identity of Galactus.

377. Laura Kinney is also known as X-23 and what superhero name?

378. Otto Octavius is better known as which villain?

   a. Dr. Octivarium

   b. The Octopus

   c. Dr. Octopus

   d. Octave Man

379. The amulet that Dr. Strange wears is known as:

   a. The Eye of Agamotto

   b. The All-Seeing Eye

   c. The Eye of the Agnostic

   d. The Eye of Infinity

380. Wolverine is also known as Logan, and which other name?

   a. James Bartlett

   b. James Howlett

   c. James Dermott

   d. James Herriott

381. Monica Rambeau, a good friend of Captain Marvel's, goes by which superhero name?

a. Pulsar
b. Spectrum
c. Neutron
d. Wavelength

382. WHAT WAS THE NAME OF THE CANADIAN MUTANT SUPERHERO TEAM THAT FIRST APPEARED IN THE X-MEN?

383. Spider-Man was created by:

a. Stan Lee
b. Stan Lee and Steve Ditko
c. Stan Lee and Jack Kirby
d. Stan Lee and Bob Kane

384. Who is the publisher of the *Daily Bugle*, who makes life rough for Peter Parker and Spider-Man?

a. J. Jeremy Jackson
b. J. Jonah Jameson
c. J. John Thompson
d. J. Jared Smithson

385. Annabelle Riggs, human ally of Valkyrie, has what job?

a. Botanist
b. Archeologist
c. Geologist
d. Dentist

386. What is Elsa Bloodstone's talent?

a. She's a leading monster historian
b. She's an expert monster-hunter
c. She's a scientist specializing in studying monster biology
d. She can control monsters with her mind

387. Ben Grimm is better known to the world as which sometimes reluctant superhero?

388. Iron Fist is one-half of which superhero duo?
a. Protectors for Fame
b. Fighters for Freedom
c. Champions for Good
d. Heroes for Hire

389. Moon Knight represents which ancient Egyptian god on earth?
a. Horus
b. Khonshu
c. Anubis
d. Ra

TOUGH TRIVIA CHALLENGE

390. Which of the following villains is best known for fighting against the Incredible Hulk?
a. The Hobgoblin
b. The Abomination
c. The Shocker
d. Ultron

391. What is Daisy Johnson's superhero name?
a. Break
b. Quake
c. Mistake
d. Shake

392. TRUE OR FALSE? BUCKY BARNES APPEARED IN THE FIRST ISSUE OF CAPTAIN AMERICA COMICS.

393. Doreen Allene Green is the secret identity of which superhero?
a. Silver Sable
b. Squirrel Girl
c. Ghost Spider
d. The Wasp

394. Which of the following is the secret identity of Ghost Rider?
a. Robbie Reyes
b. Danny Ketch
c. Johnny Blaze
d. All of the above

395. TRUE OR FALSE? THE INHUMANS ARE ANOTHER KIND OF MUTANT.

396. MILES MORALES GOES BY WHICH SUPERHERO NAME?

397. Who temporarily took on the title and powers of Thor while battling cancer?

a. May Parker   b. Jane Foster

c. Rick Jones   d. Ben Reilly

398. True or False? Spider-Man's black suit (which he obtained during *Secret Wars* adventure), was really an alien life-form that bonded with him.

399. What superhero team is known for being loved and hated equally by society?

400. How did the Fantastic Four gain their powers?

Answers: 387. The Thing; 388. d; 389. b; 390. b; 391. b; 392. True; 393. b; 394. d; 395. False, they were created through Kree experimentation on Earth; 396. Spider-Man; 397. b; 398. True; 399. The X-Men; 400. Exposure to cosmic rays while aboard a spaceship, which mutated each of them

MARVEL & DC MOVIES & TV

401. Diana (Wonder Woman) was raised on which mythical island?

a. Amazonia
b. Olympus
c. Themyscira
d. Arcadia

402. What does MCU stand for?

a. Mighty Creative Universe
b. Marvel Cinematic Universe
c. Magnificent Comics Universe
d. Marvel Comics Universe

403. TRUE OR FALSE? SARA LANCE IS MOST OFTEN KNOWN AS BLACK CANARY.

404. What did Phil Coulson call Tahiti on *Agents of S.H.I.E.L.D.*?

a. A wonderful place
b. A terrible place
c. A welcoming place
d. A magical place

405. Before she knew her true identity, Daisy Johnson (Quake) of *Agents of S.H.I.E.L.D.* went by which name?

a. Rainne   b. Ariel
c. Skye   d. Myst

406. Who is Caitlin Snow's alternate identity on the TV show *The Flash*?

a. Killer Frost
b. Savatar
c. Gypsy
d. Captain Cold

MATCH THE ACTOR WITH THE MARVEL OR DC FILM THEY APPEARED IN:

407. Jack Nicholson
408. Tobey Maguire
409. Heath Ledger
410. Ben Affleck
411. Gal Gadot
412. Zoe Saldana
413. Christopher Reeve
414. Robert Downey Jr.
415. Tessa Thompson
416. Ryan Reynolds

a. *Guardians of the Galaxy*
b. *Batman vs. Superman*
c. *Batman Returns*
d. *Deadpool*
e. *Superman (1978)*
f. *Wonder Woman*
g. *Thor: Ragnaraok*
h. *The Dark Knight*
i. *Avengers: Endgame*
j. *Spider-Man (2002)*

477. WHAT *IS* THE SECRET PHRASE *UTTERED* BY THE ENEMIES OF S.H.I.E.L.D. IN SEVERAL MCU MOVIES AND *TV* SHOWS?

418. Jefferson Pierce, the hero known as Black Lightning, started his TV series with which job?
a. Lawyer
b. High school principal
c. Security Guard
d. Police officer

419. How many superheroes were members of the Avengers team in the first Avengers MCU movie?
a. Six b. Five
c. Seven d. Eight

420. The fearsome sea creatures that Aquaman fights before finding his mother are known as what?
a. The Deep Ones   b. The Trench
c. The Fishlings   d. The Shark-men

Answers: 401. c; 402. b; 403. False, Sara Lance is White Canary; 404. d; 405. b; 406. a; 407. c; 408. j; 409. h; 410. b; 411. f; 412. a; 413. e; 414. i; 415. g; 416. d; 417. "Hail Hydra"; 418. b; 419. a; 420. b

Culture & Entertainment • 57

421. Which of the following heroes is a member of the Justice League in the movie *Justice League*?

a. Hawkman   b. Martian Manhunter

c. The Flash   d. Green Lantern

422. The name of the ship that the Legends of Tomorrow use is called which of these?

a. Energy-Raft
b. Timeboat
c. Waverider
d. Space-Searcher

423. True or false? Michael Keaton played Batman in a total of four movies.

424. Where is the TV series *Cloak and Dagger* set?

425. Superman has which nickname?

a. Man of Iron
b. Man of Gold
c. Man of Steel
d. Man of Platinum

426. What does DCEU stand for?

a. DC Expanded Universe
b. DC Extra Universe
c. DC Extended Universe
d. DC Executive Universe

427. Who played The Joker in Tim Burton's *Batman* (1989)?

a. Michael Keaton
b. Marlon Brando
c. Jack Nicholson
d. Willem Dafoe

428. The Vision's android form was originally meant to be a body for which villain?

a. Ronan
b. Loki
c. Ultron
d. Thanos

429. True or false? Star Lord's father is Ego, the Living Planet.

430. Nico Minoru's magical weapon on *Runaways* is called what?

a. The Staff of the Ancient One   b. The Wand of Infinity

c. The Staff of One   d. The Rod of Enchantment

431. Slade Wilson is which villain on the TV show *Arrow*?

a. Vigilante   b. Deathstroke   c. Black Canary   d. Deadshot

432. Maggie Sawyer, Alex's girlfriend on *Supergirl* season 2, has which job?

a. Politician   b. Scientist   c. Detective   d. Private investigator

MATCH EACH ACTOR TO THE ROLE THEY PLAYED IN A DC OR MARVEL FILM:

433. Robert Downey Jr.	a. Captain America
434. Tessa Thompson	b. Gamora
435. Christopher Reeve	c. Wolverine
436. Zoe Saldana	d. Captain Marvel
437. Heath Ledger	e. Iron Man
438. Michael Keaton	f. Superman
439. Chris Evans	g. Valkyrie
440. Brie Larson	h. Batman
441. Danai Gurira	i. The Joker
442. Hugh Jackman	j. Okoye

443. ROCKET'S TREE-LIKE ALIEN BEST FRIEND IS NAMED WHAT?

444. What is the name of the island where Oliver Queen is stranded on *Arrow*?
a. Yin Yang
b. Shanghai
c. Xanadu
d. Lian Yu

445. True or false? The Red Skull is the keeper of the Soul Stone in *Avengers: Infinity War*.

446. Who killed Brice Wayne's parents on the TV show *Gotham*?
a. Jack Napier
b. Matches Malone
c. Lex Luthor
d. Joe Chill

447. Who does Peggy Carter work for in season 1 of *Agent Carter*?

448. True or false? Jessica Jones is a police officer.

449. When Deadpool talks to the movie audience, it's a technique known as what?

450. Matt Murdock's one-time girlfriend, now an assassin, is who?
a. Giganta
b. Hektora
c. Elektra
d. Diana

DISNEY & PIXAR

451. *Brave* takes place in which country?
- a. Wales
- b. Scotland
- c. England
- d. Ireland

452. What is WALL-E's job?
- a. Scientific exploration
- b. Painter
- c. Trash collector
- d. Spaceship repair

453. True or false? Dumbo never speaks a single line in his animated film.

454. WHO CURRENTLY OWNS PIXAR?

455. What is the name of the whale who swallows Pinocchio?
- a. Tremendoso
- b. Giganto
- c. Monstro
- d. Moby-Dick

456. What is Jasmine's pet tiger's name in *Aladdin*?
- a. Mustafa
- b. Scar
- c. Rajah
- d. Baloo

TOUGH TRIVIA CHALLENGE

457. TRUE OR FALSE? BING BONG IS RILEY'S ENEMY IN INSIDE OUT.

Answers: 444. d; 445. True; 446. b; 447. The Strategic Scientific Reserve; 448. False, she is a private investigator; 449. Breaking the fourth wall; 450. c; 451. b; 452. c; 453. True; 454. Disney; 455. c; 456. c; 457. False, Bing Bong is Riley's imaginary friend

458. Riley plays what sport in *Inside Out?*

a. Soccer

b. Basketball

c. Hockey

d. Baseball

459. Which Disney princess has a star on Hollywood's Walk of Fame?

a. Ariel

b. Belle

c. Snow White

d. Cinderella

MATCH THE FOLLOWING DISNEY HERO/PRINCESS TO THEIR ANIMATED MOVIE:

460. Belle

461. Vanellope Von Schweetz

462. Ariel

463. Pongo

464. Merida

465. Prince Philip

466. Elsa

467. Esmeralda

468. Rapunzel

469. Baymax

a. *101 Dalmatians*

b. *The Hunchback of Notre Dame*

c. *Big Hero 6*

d. *Beauty and the Beast*

e. *Wreck-It Ralph*

f. *Sleeping Beauty*

g. *The Little Mermaid*

h. *Frozen*

i. *Brave*

j. *Tangled*

470. In *Peter Pan* what are the names of the three Darling children?

471. Who wrote the original book of *The Hunchback of Notre-Dame*?

a. Lord Byron

b. Victor Hugo

c. Charles Dickens

d. Mary Shelley

472. In *Robin Hood*, what kind of animal is the minstrel, Alan-a-Dale?

   a. Fox
   b. Bear
   c. Mouse
   d. Rooster

473. Where do Mufasa and his family live in *The Lion King*?

   a. Lion's Den
   b. Pride Rock
   c. Cat Gulch
   d. Pride Mountain

474. Billy Crystal is the voice for which character in *Monsters Inc.*?

   a. Randy
   b. Sulley
   c. Mike
   d. Boo

475. True or False? In *Brave*, fairies lead Merida to the witch.

476. Which Disney animated film was originally shown in only 14 theaters around the world?

477. What is the skunk's name in *Bambi*?

   a. Flower
   b. Blossom
   c. Orchid
   d. Rose

478. What is the name of Maleficent's raven?

   a. Malice
   b. Diabolo
   c. Inferno
   d. Poe

TOUGH TRIVIA CHALLENGE

479. True or false? Mickey Mouse was the first cartoon character to be honored with a star on Hollywood's Walk of Fame.

MATCH THE FOLLOWING PIXAR VILLAINS TO THEIR MOVIES:

480. Lotso	a. Coco
481. Professor Zündapp	b. The Incredibles
482. Ernesto de la Cruz	c. Toy Story 3
483. Stinky Pete	d. Ratatouille
484. Randall Boggs	e. Cars 2
485. Hopper	f. Monsters Inc.
486. Mor'du	g. Toy Story 2
487. Sid	h. Toy Story
488. Syndrome	i. A Bug's Life
489. Chef Skinner	j. Brave

490. HOW OLD IS SNOW WHITE IN THE STORY?

491. Whose name is written on the sole of Woody's boot in *Toy Story*?

a. Randy   b. Andy   c. Jesse   d. Buzz

492. Who goes on a high-flying adventure in *Up*?
a. Carl Fredricksen
b. Cal Ferguson
c. Cole Freddies
d. Frederick Carlson

493. Ratatouille is set in which European city?
a. London
b. Rome
c. Brussels
d. Paris

494. Which Disney animated film was the first to receive an Oscar nomination for Best Picture?
   a. Pinocchio
   b. Beauty and the Beast
   c. The Little Mermaid
   d. Aladdin

TOUGH TRIVIA CHALLENGE

495. TRUE OR FALSE? PIXAR'S FIRST FEATURE FILM WAS TOY STORY.

496. What does Dumbo use in order to fly?
   a. A feather   b. His ears   c. His tail   d. His legs

497. WHO IS THE ONLY DISNEY PRINCESS WHO HAS BROTHERS?

498. Where do the toys end up being trapped in *Toy Story 3*?
   a. Sunnyside Daycare   b. Poppy's Primary School
   c. Sunnyside Retirement Home d. Daisy Daycare

499. What type of fish is Nemo?
         a. Salmon   b. Blue-tang fish
         c. Clown fish   d. Gold fish

500. Remy the rat dreams of what in *Ratatouille*?
      a. Going home   b. Learning French
      c. Saving his friends   d. Becoming a great chef

MORE COMICS

501. In Calvin and Hobbes, Calvin's stuffed, imaginary friend Hobbes is what kind of animal?
a. Dog   b. Bear
c. Tiger   d. Lion

502. In *Archie Comics*, what is Jughead's real name?
a. Max
b. Dennis
c. Forsythe
d. Archibald

503. In *Bloom County*, Opus is what kind of animal?
a. Otter
b. Penguin
c. Parrot
d. Basset hound

504. TRUE OR FALSE? POPEYE GETS HIS STRENGTH FROM CARROTS.

MATCH THE FOLLOWING COMIC STRIP CHARACTERS TO THEIR PROFESSIONS:

505. Henry Mitchell, father of Dennis the Menace
506. Broom Hilda
507. Dagwood Bumstead
508. Hägar the Horrible
509. Popeye
510. Beetle Bailey
511. Mike Doonesbury
512. Charlie Brown's father
513. Dick Tracy
514. Brenda Starr

a. Barber
b. Office manager
c. Internet sales
d. Police detective
e. Viking
f. Aerospace engineer
g. Army private
h. Sailor
i. Witch
j. Newspaper reporter

515. MARMADUKE IS WHAT KIND OF ANIMAL?

▲▲▲▲▲▲▲▲▲▲▲▲▲▲▲

516. In *Calvin and Hobbes*, what are Calvin's parents' names?

a. Luther and Rene

b. The dad is Henry, the mom's name is not given

c. Edward and Elizabeth

d. We never learn their names

▲▲▲▲▲▲▲▲▲▲▲▲▲▲▲

517. In *Archie Comics*, which two are always fighting over Archie?

a. Karen and Veronica

b. Betty and Veronica

c. Susie and Madeline

d. Betty and Janet

▲▲▲▲▲▲▲▲▲▲▲▲▲▲▲

518. In *Bloom County*, Steve Dallas has what job?

a. Lawyer   b. Doctor

c. Reporter   d. Store manager

519. True or false? *Gareld* is the most widely-syndicated comic strip in the world.

▲▲▲▲▲▲▲▲▲▲▲▲▲▲▲

520. In *Peanuts*, who does Linus wait for every Halloween?

a. The Great Ghost

b. The Headless Horseman

c. The Great Pumpkin

d. The Bringer of Candy

521. In *Calvin and Hobbes*, Calvin is known for making what kind of horrifying creations?

a. Snowmen

b. Mud pies

c. Pencil artwork

d. Blanket forts

522. In *Bloom County*, Bill the Cat is a spoof of what other cartoon cat?

a. Sylvester   b. Felix

c. Garfield   d. Heathcliff

523. What is the name of the dimwitted dog in the *Garfield* comic strip?

524. In *Peanuts*, what service does Lucy offer for five cents?
a. Physical therapy
b. Car washing
c. Math tutoring
d. Psychiatric help

525. In *Calvin and Hobbes*, which girl is Calvin's self-described enemy?
a. Kim
b. Susie
c. Mary
d. Gwen

526. In *Bloom County*, what does Binkley have in his room that always concerns him?
a. A worry chest
b. An anger wardrobe
c. A boredom bookshelf
d. An anxiety closet

527. In *Peanuts*, Schroeder plays what instrument?
a. Piano
b. Guitar
c. Drums
d. Flute

528. True or false? The first newspaper comic strips appeared in the late 19th century.

Match the following comic characters with their spouses or partners (current or former):

529. Elly Patterson *(For Better or for Worse)*
530. Olive Oyl
531. Alice *(Dennis the Menace)*
532. Lois
533. Blondie
534. Lola Granola *(Bloom County)*
535. Loretta Lockhorn
536. Sally Forth
537. Loweezy
538. Florrie

a. Popeye
b. Leroy
c. John
d. Henry Mitchell
e. Andy Capp
f. Dagwood Bumstead
g. Hi
h. Ted
i. Snuffy Smith
j. Opus

539. WHAT IS THE NAME OF THE BIRD WHO IS SNOOPY'S BEST FRIEND?

540. In *Bloom County*, what classic TV show do Cutter John and the others like to pretend they are in?
   a. Gilligan's Island
   b. Star Trek
   c. The A-Team
   d. M*A*S*H

541. In *Archie Comics*, where are most of the stories set?
   a. Glendale
   b. Point Pleasant
   c. Ingburgh
   d. Riverdale

Answers: 523. Odie; 524. d; 525. b; 526. d; 527. a; 528. True; 529. c; 530. a; 531. d; 532. g; 533. f; 534. j; 535. b; 536. h; 537. i; 538. e; 539. Woodstock; 540. b; 541. d

542. In *Calvin and Hobbes*, Calvin daydreams about being which science fiction hero?
- a. Spaceman Biff
- b. Captain Galaxy
- c. Spaceman Spiff
- d. Commander Starr

543. In *Archie Comics*, who is always chasing after Jughead?
- a. Doris
- b. Amy
- c. Candie
- d. Ethel

544. TRUE OR FALSE? DOONESBURY WAS THE FIRST COMIC STRIP TO WIN A PULITZER PRIZE

545. In the comic strip *Pearls before Swine*, who are the crocs always trying to get?

546. In *Peanuts*, who is Charlie Brown's younger sister?
- a. Violet
- b. Lucy
- c. Sally
- d. Patty

547. True or false? *The Far Side* was created by Jerry Larson.

548. WHO DOES SNOOPY IMAGINE HE'S FIGHTING IN A WORLD WAR I BIPLANE?

549. In *Peanuts*, what does Marcie call Peppermint Patty?
- a. Ma'am
- b. Sir
- c. Miss
- d. Mister

550. In *Archie Comics*, who is the famous local singer and her band?
- a. Amy and the Alley Cats
- b. Josie and the Pussycats
- c. Becky and the Beasts
- d. Josie and the Puppies

•MOVIES•

ACTION & ADVENTURE

551. In the *Lethal Weapon* movies, Murtaugh was played by which actor?
a. Will Smith
b. Denzel Washington
c. Danny Glover
d. Eddie Murphy

552. Rambo was a veteran of which war?
a. Afghanistan
b. Vietnam
c. The Gulf War
d. World War II

553. Which actor has played James Bond?
a. Timothy Dalton
b. George Lazenby
c. Daniel Craig
d. All of the above

554. True or false? Clint Eastwood starred in five *Dirty Harry* movies.

555. The movie *The Rock* is set in which prison?
a. Attica
b. San Quentin
c. Alcatraz
d. Leavenworth

556. What kind of animal is Indiana Jones afraid of?
a. Spiders
b. Snakes
c. Tigers
d. Bats

Answers: 542. c; 543. d; 544. True; 545. Zebra; 546. c; 547. False, it was created by Gary Larson; 548. The Red Baron; 549. b; 550. b; 551. c; 552. b; 553. d; 554. True; 555. c; 556. b.

Culture & Entertainment • 71

557. TRUE OR FALSE? THE ROBOCOP MOVIES ARE SET IN A FUTURISTIC NEW YORK.

MATCH THE FOLLOWING ACTION MOVIES WITH THEIR DIRECTORS:

558. *Kingsman: The Secret Service*
559. *Mad Max: Fury Road*
560. *Lethal Weapon (1987)*
561. *The Fast and the Furious (2001)*
562. *John Wick*
563. *Die Hard (1988)*
564. *Tomb Raider (2018)*
565. *The Terminator (1984)*
566. *Sherlock Holmes: A Game of Shadows (2011)*
567. *Mission Impossible: Fallout*

a. George Miller
b. Chad Stahelski
c. Guy Ritchie
d. Christopher McQuarrie
e. Matthew Vaughn
f. Richard Donner
g. Roar Uthaug
h. Rob Cohen
i. James Cameron
j. John McTiernan

568. Mel Gibson plays which historical hero in *Braveheart*?

a. William Wallace
b. Robert the Bruce
c. King Edward
d. Prince Edward

569. Who is the main villain in the first *Die Hard* movie?

a. Hans Schmidt
b. Argyle
c. Hans Gruber
d. Richard Thornburg

570. True or false? In *Red Dawn*, a group of teenagers try to save their town from invading Soviet forces.

571. WHAT IS THE FIRST RULE OF FIGHT CLUB?

572. In *The Hunger Games*, Katniss comes from which District of Panem?
a. Three   b. Twelve   c. Nine   d. One

573. The cop Dirty Harry works in which city?

a. New York   b. San Francisco   c. Los Angeles   d. Miami

MATCH THE FOLLOWING ACTORS TO THE ACTION MOVIES IN WHICH THEY HAD LEAD ROLES:

574. Bruce Lee   **a.** *xXx*

575. Mel Gibson   **b.** *Atomic Blonde*

576. The Rock (Dwane Johnson)   **c.** *Lethal Weapon*

577. Vin Diesel   **d.** *Tomb Raider (2018)*

578. Tom Cruise   **e.** *Skyfall*

579. Alicia Vikander   **f.** *Rush Hour*

580. Jackie Chan   **g.** *Enter the Dragon*

581. Bruce Willis   **h.** *The Fate of the Furious*

582. Charlize Theron   **i.** *Mission Impossible: Rogue Nation*

583. Daniel Craig   **j.** *Die Hard*

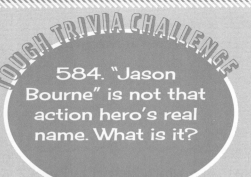

584. "Jason Bourne" is not that action hero's real name. What is it?

585. Arnold Schwarzenegger plays Colonel John Matrix in which movie?
a. *Rambo*
b. *Commando*
c. *True Lies*
d. *Total Recall*

586. TRUE OR FALSE? THE FIRST *DIE HARD* FILM IS SET DURING THE FOURTH OF JULY.

587. WHAT'S THE NAME OF THE MOVIE SERIES THAT BRINGS BACK LOADS OF ACTION HEROES FROM THE 1980S?

MATCH THE FOLLOWING MOVIES WITH THE ACTOR THAT STARRED IN THEM:

588. *Die Hard*
589. *Olympus Has Fallen*
590. *John Wick*
591. *Fast & Furious: Hobbs & Shaw*
592. *The Bourne Supremacy*
593. *Speed*
594. *Lara Croft: Tomb Raider*
595. *Robocop*
596. *Mission: Impossible – Ghost Protocol*
597. *Kingsman: The Golden Circle*

a. Jason Statham
b. Sandra Bullock
c. Keanu Reeves
d. Bruce Willis
e. Colin Firth
f. Angelina Jolie
g. Gerard Butler
h. Matt Damon
i. Tom Cruise
j. Peter Weller

598. True or false? Daniel Craig's first James Bond film was *Casino Royale*, in 2006.

599. WHO DIRECTED *CROUCHING TIGER, HIDDEN DRAGON?*

600. *Saving Private Ryan* was set during which major historical battle?

SCI-FI, FANTASY & HORROR

601. What is Gollum's original name in *The Lord of The Rings?*
- a. Peregrin
- b. Smeagol
- c. Samwise
- d. Pippin

602. In *Harry Potter and the Chamber of Secrets*, what monster is released from the Chamber of Secrets?
- a. Manticore
- b. Troll
- c. Dragon
- d. Basilisk

603. Complete the phrase from *Harry Potter and the Prisoner of Azkaban*: I solemnly swear . . .
- a. That I am up to no good
- b. To behave
- c. To tell the truth
- d. To serve Hogwarts loyally

604. THE NA'VI WOMAN THAT JAKE SULLY FALLS IN LOVE WITH IN *AVATAR* IS NAMED WHAT?
- A. TSU'TEY
- B. EYTUKAN
- C. MO'AT
- D. NEYTIRI

Answers: 584. David Webb; 585. b; 586. False, it takes place during Christmas; 587. *The Expendables*; 588. d; 589. g; 590. c; 591. a; 592. h; 593. b; 594. f; 595. j; 596. i; 597. e; 598. True; 599. Ang Lee; 600. D-Day, the Normandy Invasion; 601. b; 602. d; 603. a; 604. d

605. What is the name of the cute Mogwai in *Gremlins*?
- a. Grumpy
- b. Gadget
- c. Gizmo
- d. Gordon

606. True or false? Eowyn is slain by the Witch-king in *Return of the King.*

MATCH THE FOLLOWING SCIENCE FICTION MOVIES WITH THEIR DIRECTORS:

607. *Back to the Future*
608. *Star Wars Episode V: The Empire Strikes Back*
609. *THX 1138*
610. *Blade Runner*
611. *Metropolis*
612. *Close Encounters of the Third Kind*
613. *The Matrix*
614. *Avatar*
615. *Star Wars Episode VII: The Force Awakens*
616. *2001: A Space Odyssey*

- a. George Lucas
- b. Steven Spielberg
- c. J.J. Abrams
- d. Fritz Lang
- e. Robert Zemeckis
- f. Stanley Kubrick
- g. The Wachowskis
- h. Irvin Kershner
- i. Ridley Scott
- j. James Cameron

617. In *Willow*, who is Bavmorda's main servant?

618. The angry spirit in *The Ring* is named what?
- a. Kara b. Samara
- c. Harra d. Mala

619. What famous line does the little girl, Carol Anne, say in *Poltergeist*?

a. Run away   **b. Help me**   **c. They're here**   **d. Go away**

620. True or false? The Vulcan home world is destroyed in *Star Trek* (2009).

621. Who played the title role in 2004's *Van Helsing*?

622. The tiny, bird-like creatures that live with Luke Skywalker on Ahch-To in *Star Wars Episode VIII: The Last Jedi* are called what?

a. Borgs   b. Jawas   c. Porgs   d. Banthas

623. In *Star Wars: A New Hope*, at which docking bay did Luke and Ben agree to meet Han Solo?

a. 41   b. 62   c. 94   d. 173

624. In *Lord of the Rings: Fellowship of the Ring*, which of these Hobbits are Bilbo's enemies?

a. The Proudfeet   b. The Sackville-Bagginses
c. The Tooks   d. The Brandybucks

625. True or false? The Death Eaters in Harry Potter are ghosts who take vengeance on the living.

▲▲▲▲▲▲▲▲▲▲▲▲▲▲▲▲▲▲▲▲▲▲▲▲▲▲▲

MATCH THE FOLLOWING FANTASY MOVIES WITH THEIR DIRECTORS:

626. *The Lord of the Rings*
627. *Labyrinth*
628. *Alice in Wonderland* (2010)
629. *Harry Potter and the Prisoner of Azkaban*
630. *The Chronicles of Narnia: The Lion, the Witch and the Wardrobe* (2005)
631. *Willow*
632. *Pan's Labyrinth*
633. *Legend*
634. *The Adventures of Baron Munchausen* (1988)
635. *The Princess Bride*

a. Ridley Scott
b. Rob Reiner
c. Tim Burton
d. Peter Jackson
e. Jim Henson
f. Guillermo del Toro
g. Alfonso Cuaron
h. Andrew Adamson
i. Terry Gilliam
j. Ron Howard

▲▲▲▲▲▲▲▲▲▲▲▲▲▲▲▲▲▲▲▲▲▲▲▲▲▲▲

636. WHAT *IS* THE PLACE THAT THE DWARVES *IN THE HOBBIT* ARE TRYING TO TAKE BACK?

▲▲▲▲▲▲▲▲▲▲▲▲▲▲▲▲▲▲▲▲▲▲▲▲▲▲▲

637. True or false? In *Star Wars*, Kylo Ren was originally named Ben Kenobi.

MATCH THE FOLLOWING FANTASY MOVIE ACTORS WITH THEIR CHARACTERS:

638. Ian McKellan
639. Warwick Davis
640. Mia Sara
641. Martin Freeman
642. Robin Wright
643. Rupert Grint
644. Dominic Monaghan
645. Tilda Swinton
646. Evanna Lynch
647. Miranda Otto

a. Eowyn
b. Merry
c. Bilbo
d. Willow
e. Princess Lili
f. Gandalf
g. Buttercup
h. Jadis, the White Witch
i. Ron Weasley
j. Luna Lovegood

648. What is the emperor's name in *Star Wars*?

649. In the movie *Dune*, what is another name for the planet Arrakis?

650. TRUE OR FALSE? PAUL ATREIDES *IS* THE MAIN HERO OF THE MOVIE *DUNE*.

Answers: 626. d; 627. e; 628. c; 629. g; 630. h; 631. j; 632. f; 633. a; 634. i; 635. b; 635. False, they are followers of Voldemort; 636. The Lonely Mountain; 637. False, his name was Ben Solo; 638. f; 639. d; 640. e; 641. c; 642. g; 643. i; 644. b; 645. h; 646. j; 647. a; 648. Palpatine; 649. Dune; 650. True.

•TV•

COMEDY

651. On *Brooklyn Nine-Nine*, Rosa Diaz secretly has which dancing skill?

  a. Jazz   b. Salsa
  c. Ballet d. Square Dancing

652. Max Black and Caroline Channing are waitresses on which comedy?

  a. *How I Met Your Mother*
  b. *2 Broke Girls*
  c. *Alice*
  d. *Wonderfalls*

653. On *Cheers*, Sam Malone played which baseball position for the Boston Red Sox?

  a. Outfield
  b. Second Base
  c. Pitcher
  d. Catcher

654. On *The Good Place*, Tahani has a big rivalry with who?

  a. Her mother
  b. Her brother
  c. Her sister
  d. Her childhood best friend

655. TRUE OR FALSE? ON EVERYBODY LOVES RAYMOND, RAYMOND'S LAST NAME IS BARONE.

MATCH EACH ACTOR OR ACTRESS TO THE COMEDY SHOW THEY STARRED IN:

656. Florence Henderson
657. David Hyde Pierce
658. Michael Richards
659. Mila Kunis
660. Matthew Perry
661. Rainn Wilson
662. Tracy Morgan
663. Rhea Perlman
664. Mike Farrell
665. John Ritter

a. *The Office* (American version)
b. *Cheers*
c. *Three's Company*
d. *That '70s Show*
e. *Frasier*
f. *Friends*
g. *The Brady Bunch*
h. *Seinfeld*
i. *M*A*S*H*
j. *30 Rock*

666. ON *CHEERS*, WHAT DOES EVERYBODY KNOW?

667. On *Married with Children*, what does Al sell for a living?
a. Shoes   b. Computers
c. Cars   d. Propane

668. On *Modern Family*, where is Gloria from?
a. Ecuador
b. Colombia
c. Chile
d. Brazil

TOUGH TRIVIA CHALLENGE

669. On *Will & Grace*, what is one of Karen's favorite phrases?
a. Oh baby
b. Oh no
c. Oh dear
d. Oh honey

Answers: 651. c; 652. b; 653. c; 654. c; 655. True; 656. g; 657. e; 658. h; 659. d; 660. f; 661. a; 662. j; 663. b; 664. i; 665. c; 666. Your name; 667. a; 668. b; 669. d

Culture & Entertainment • 81

670. On *Seinfeld*, Jerry lives where?

   a. The Upper East Side
   b. The Lower West Side
   c. The Upper West Side
   d. The Lower East Side

671. On *The Simpsons*, who is Homer's boss?

   a. Waylon Smithers
   b. Nelson Muntz
   c. Ned Flanders
   d. Mr. Burns

672. True or false? On *3rd Rock From the Sun*, the aliens live in Cleveland, Ohio.

673. On *Newhart*, what are the names of the three brothers?

674. On *30 Rock*, what does Jack put on at 6 pm each day?

   a. A tie
   b. A tuxedo
   c. A bathrobe
   d. Shoes

675. Which *Friends* character wrote the song "Smelly Cat"?

   a. Chandler
   b. Monica
   c. Phoebe
   d. Ross

676. On *Frasier*, who is Niles Crane's never-seen wife, about whom Niles always has a story to tell?

   a. Roz
   b. Maris
   c. Stacy
   d. Daphne

677. True or false? *Monty Python's Flying Circus* began life as a stage show.

678. ON *BROOKLYN NINE-NINE*, WHAT IS THE ANNUAL TRADITION THE PRECINCT CELEBRATES?

679. On *The Simpsons*, what are the names of Marge's sisters?
a. Lisa and Maggie
b. Patty and Selma
c. Maude and Sally
d. Thelma and Louise

680. True or false? Frasier Crane hosts a television show.

MATCH THE FOLLOWING SUPPORTING CHARACTERS TO THEIR SITCOMS:

681. Bernadette Rostenkowski-Wolowitz
682. Han Lee
683. Lilith Sternin
684. Fez
685. Tom Haverford
686. Ginger Grant
687. Zoey Johnson
688. Joanie Cunningham
689. Gina Lonetti
690. Woody Boyd

a. *2 Broke Girls*
b. *Parks and Recreation*
c. *Happy Days*
d. *Cheers*
e. *Big Bang Theory*
f. *Cheers*
g. *Gilligan's Island*
h. *Brooklyn Nine-Nine*
i. *That '70s Show*
j. *Black-ish*

691. Who is the dim-witted sidekick on the British comedy *Blackadder*?

Answers: 670. c; 671. d; 672. False, they live in Rutherford, Ohio; 673. Larry, Darryl, and Darryl; 674. b; 675. c; 676. b; 677. False, it began as the comedy broadcast series; 678. The Halloween Heist; 679. b; 680. False, he hosts a radio show; 681. e; 682. a; 683. f; 684. i; 685. b; 686. g; 687. j; 688. c; 689. h; 690. d; 691. Baldrick

Culture & Entertainment • 83

692. On *King of Queens*, who does Doug Heffernan work for?
   a. UPS
   b. USPS
   c. IPS
   d. DHL

693. On *Parks and Recreation*, what is Leslie's favorite food?
   a. Chocolate
   b. Pancakes
   c. Waffles
   d. Ice cream

694. On *The Big Bang Theory*, what instrument does Sheldon play?
   a. Accordion   b. Flute
   c. Guitar   d. Theremin

695. What type of restaurant is seen most often on *The Good Place*?
   a. Hamburger
   b. Chinese
   c. Frozen yogurt
   d. Pizza

696. On *How I Met Your Mother*, what is the name of the bar where the five friends always like to hang out?
   a. The Scene
   b. Barney's
   c. MacLaren's Pub
   d. O'Donnell's Pub

697. Which body part appears at the end of the opening credits of *Monty Python's Flying Circus*?

698. On *That '70s Show*, who is the dimwitted member of the group who likes to talk about how good-looking he is?
   a. Hyde
   b. Red
   c. Kelso
   d. Fez

699. On *The Office* (American version), what kind of movies are shown on Movie Mondays?

a. Old musicals
b. Westerns
c. Horror films
d. Training videos

TOUGH TRIVIA CHALLENGE

700. TRUE OR FALSE? ON FRIENDS, MONICA AND ROSS ARE COUSINS.

DRAMA

701. *Downton Abbey* is set in which English county?

a. Shropshire
b. Yorkshire
c. Derbyshire
d. Oxfordshire

702. Lorelai Gilmore owns what establishment?

a. The Hartford Cafe
b. Luke's Diner
c. The Dragonfly Inn
d. The Stars Hollow B&B

703. On *Grey's Anatomy*, which of these is the intern's nickname for Meredith?

a. Your Highness
b. Vampira
c. Medusa
d. Cruella

704. *Mad men* is set in which kind of business?

a. A newspaper
b. A law firm
c. An advertising agency
d. A factory

705. TRUE OR FALSE? *GLEE* IS SET IN WILLIAM MCKINLEY HIGH SCHOOL IN LIMA, OHIO.

MATCH THE FOLLOWING CHARACTERS TO THEIR TV DRAMA SHOWS:

706. Kurt Hummel	a. The Good Wife
707. Blair Waldorf	b. The West Wing
708. Brooke Davis	c. House
709. Luke Danes	d. The Wire
710. Dylan McKay	e. NCIS
711. Robert Crawley	f. One Tree Hill
712. Alicia Florrick	g. Grey's Anatomy
713. Cristina Yang	h. Gilmore Girls
714. June Osborne	i. The Crown
715. Elizabeth Jennings	j. The Sopranos
716. Winston Churchill	k. Glee
717. Dr. Eric Foreman	l. The Americans
718. Carrie Mathison	m. Beverly Hills 90210
719. Leroy Jethro Gibbs	n. Gossip Girl
720. Don Draper	o. Downton Abbey
721. Claire Underwood	p. Handmaid's Tale
722. Josiah "Jed" Bartlet	q. Law and Order
723. Jack McCoy	r. Homeland
724. Dr. Jennifer Melfi	s. House of Cards
725. Bunk Moreland	t. Madmen

726. *The Sopranos* takes place mainly in which state?
a. New York   b. New Jersey
c. Pennsylvania d. Connecticut

727. On *Homeland*, where had Brody been held prisoner?
  a. Iran
  b. Russia
  c. Iraq
  d. Pakistan

728. On *The Americans*, Elizabeth and Philip Jennings work for which organization?
  a. The CIA
  b. The KGB
  c. The FBI
  d. The GPU

729. True or false? On *Beverly Hills 90210*, Brandon and Brenda Walsh are twins.

730. In *Pretty Little Liars*, Emily is great at which sport?
  a. Gymnastics
  b. Softball
  c. Basketball
  d. Swimming

731. Which famous actor had a long-running early role on the show ER?
  a. Jim Carrey
  b. Hugh Laurie
  c. Mark Harmon
  d. George Clooney

732. True or false? *The Crown* is able to film on location at Buckingham Palace.

733. WHAT *IS* THE NAME OF THE FICTIONAL COUNTRY WERE *THE HANDMAID'S TALE* IS SET?

734. *The Good Wife* is set in which city?
  a. Chicago
  b. Los Angeles
  c. Atlanta
  d. Boston

735. True or false? On *House*, Dr. Gregory House walks with a cane because he once broke his leg.

- -

MATCH THE FOLLOWING ACTORS TO THEIR FAMOUS DRAMATIC TV ROLES:

736. James Gandolfini   a. J.R. Ewing
737. Hugh Laurie   b. Dr. Gregory House
738. Lauren Graham   c. Emily Fields
739. Michelle Dockery   d. Tony Soprano
740. Christina Hendricks   e. Joan Holloway
741. Matthew Rhys   f. Lorelai Gilmore
742. Larry Hagman   g. Dr. Meredith Grey
743. Ellen Pompeo   h. Lady Mary Crawley
744. Shay Mitchell   i. Philip Jennings
745. Lea Michele   j. Rachel Berry

- -

746. On *One Tree Hill*, what is Peyton's record label called?

747. True or false? On *Gossip Girl*, Blair Waldorf sometimes dreams she is in Audrey Hepburn movies.

- -

748. WHAT DOES "NCIS" STAND FOR?

749. On *Hill Street Blues*, what was Sgt. Phil Esterhaus' famous phrase every morning?

TOUGH TRIVIA CHALLENGE

750. On the original *Law and Order*, which New York police precinct do the detectives work in?

NERD & GEEK GENRES

751. What is the name of Xena's weapon on *Xena*?
   a. Stiletto
   b. Chakram
   c. Gordion Blade
   d. Bite

753. What does the "S" in "S.H.I.E.L.D." stand for?
   a. Sudden
   b. Scientific
   c. Strategic
   d. Super

752. In *Buffy the Vampire Slayer*, what is unique about the vampire, Angel?
   a. He is not immortal
   b. He has a soul
   c. He has wings
   d. He can walk in sunlight

754. ON *THE RUNAWAYS*, WHAT IS THE NAME OF GERT'S DINOSAUR?
   A. OLD MAID
   B. LACIE
   C. OLD LACE
   D. GRACE

Answers: 735. False, he suffers from chronic pain; 736. d; 737. b; 738. f; 739. b; 740. e; 741. i; 742. a; 743. g; 744. c; 745. j; 746. Red Bedroom Records; 747. True; 748. Naval Criminal Investigative Service; 749. "Let's be careful out there."; 750. The 27th; 751. b; 752. b; 753. b; 754. c.

755. On the CW show *Arrow*, which of these completes Arrow's famous line? "You have failed . . ."
a. this country
b. my company
c. this city
d. my family

756. On *Enterprise*, what alien race is Dr. Phlox?
a. Ferengi
b. Vulcan
c. Arcturan
d. Denobulan

▲ ▲ ▲ ▲ ▲ ▲ ▲ ▲ ▲ ▲ ▲ ▲ ▲ ▲

757. True or false? Xena and Callisto are close friends.

▲ ▲

MATCH THE FOLLOWING ACTORS AND ACTRESSES TO THE TV ROLES THEY ARE FAMOUS FOR PLAYING:

758. Sarah Michelle Gellar	**a.** Clark Kent
759. Patrick Stewart	**b.** Sam Winchester
760. Nathan Fillion	**c.** Damon Salvatore
761. Melissa Benoist	**d.** Oliver Queen/Green Arrow
762. Lucy Lawless	**e.** Buffy the Vampire Slayer
763. Tom Welling	**f.** Zari Tomaz
764. KJ Apa	**g.** Iris West
765. Eliza Taylor	**h.** Clarke Griffin
766. Nafessa Williams	**i.** Captain Malcolm Reynolds
767. Stephen Amell	**j.** Lois Lane
768. Chyler Leigh	**k.** Angel
769. Jared Padalecki	**l.** Supergirl
770. Tala Ashe	**m.** Cordelia Chase
771. Charisma Carpenter	**n.** Alex Danvers
772. Avery Brooks	**o.** Archie Andrews
773. Teri Hatcher	**p.** Xena
774. Michael Hurst	**q.** Iolaus
775. David Boreanaz	**r.** Captain Jean Luc Picard
776. Candice Patton	**s.** Anissa Pierce/Thunder
777. Ian Somerhalder	**t.** Captain Benjamin Sisko

778. What is Eleven's real name on *Stranger Things*?

▲▲▲▲▲▲▲▲▲▲▲▲▲

779. *Enterprise* takes place in what century?

a. Twenty-first   b. Twenty-fourth

c. Twenty-second   d. Twenty-third

▲▲▲▲▲▲▲▲▲▲▲▲▲

780. How many seasons did *Star Trek: The Next Generation* run?

a. Six
b. Four
c. Seven
d. Five

▲▲▲▲▲▲▲▲▲▲▲▲▲

781. What popular fast food chain is in several CW DC shows?

a. Tennessee Fried Chicken
b. Joe's
c. Big Belly Burger
d. The Perfect Pizza

782. In which century is Star *Trek: The Next Generation* set?

a. Twenty-third   b. Twenty-fourth

c. Twenty-fifth   d. Twenty-second

▲▲▲▲▲▲▲▲▲▲▲▲▲

783. Which *Star Trek: The Next Generation* regular character went on to join the cast of *Deep Space Nine*?

a. Wesley Crusher
b. Worf
c. Deanna Troi
d. Data

784. In *Enterprise*, who are the time-traveling aliens that are the enemies of the Enterprise crew?

a. The Cylons
b. The Suliban
c. The Jem'Hadar
d. The Dominion

785. True or false? On *Battlestar Galactica*, the "Final Five" are a group of human-looking Cylons.

786. Who created the robot-looking Cylons on *Battlestar Galactica*?

__ __ __ __ __ __ __

787. On *Enterprise*, Hoshi Sato has what job?

    a. Second in Command

    b. Lead Engineer

    c. Communications Officer

    d. Head of Security

788. In *Buffy the Vampire Slayer*, what is the name of the demon that can make everyone sing?

    a. Cool   **b. Sweet**

    c. Prancer   **d. Tap**

789. What kind of unusual being is Daisy Johnson (Quake) on *Agents of S.H.I.E.L.D.?*

    a. Fairy   **b. Inhuman**

    c. Mutant   **d. Alien**

790. On Marvel's Runaways, what are Chase's weapons called?

    a. Fists of Fury   **b. Hand Blades**

    c. Fistigons   **d. Brass Knuckles**

791. The Romulans are related to which other alien race?

    a. The Bajorans   b. The Vulcans

    c. The Klingons   d. The Ferengi

__ __ __ __ __ __ __ __

792. On *Deep Space Nine*, the Bajoran planet was occupied for half a century by who?

    a. The Romulans   b. The Klingons

    c. The Dominion   d. The Cardassians

793. On *The Flash*, Barry Allen accidentally created another timeline called what?

a. Flashearth
b. Flashpoint
c. Flashland
d. Flashtime

794. On the CW DC shows, the aliens who invaded earth 1, requiring a big superhero team-up to stop them, were called what?

a. The Kryptonians
b. The Dominators
c. The Daxamites
d. The Skrulls

795. Who says this line: "Resistance is futile"?

a. The Cardassians
b. The Dominion
c. The Borg
d. The Klingons

796. The Deep Space Nine station is near what space phenomenon?

a. A brown dwarf
b. A neutron star
c. A worm hole
d. A black hole

TOUGH TRIVIA CHALLENGE

797. Who was the first known Inhuman on *Agents of S.H.I.E.L.D.?*
a. Jiaying
b. Lash
c. Hive
d. Magneto

798. On *Xena*, what was Gabrielle's original main weapon?

a. Dagger   b. Sword
c. Staff   d. Bow and arrow

799. In *Buffy the Vampire Slayer*, Spike and Drusilla are which of these?

a. Vampires
b. Demons
c. Buffy's best friends
d. Buffy's parents

800. What is the nickname of Agent Coulson's red corvette on *Agents of S.H.I.E.L.D.*?

a. Mira b. Lola

c. Mona d. Cara

801. IN FIREFLY, WHAT ARE THE MYSTERIOUS ENEMIES WHO LIVE AT THE OUTER EDGES OF THE SOLAR SYSTEM CALLED?

802. On *Star Trek*, what is Captain Kirk's middle name?

803. TRUE OR FALSE? SERENITY IS A FIREFLY-CLASS SPACESHIP.

804. On season three of *Enterprise*, who were trying to destroy earth because they felt humans were a threat to their own existence?

a. The Vulcans b. The Xindi

c. The Borg d. The Andorians

805. On *Star Trek: Voyager*, who is *Voyager's* captain?

a. Sisko

b. Janeway

c. Pike

d. Sulu

806. Which supernatural being appeared in season four of *Agents of S.H.I.E.L.D.*?

a. Mephisto

b. Dormammu

c. Thor

d. Ghost Rider

807. In *Buffy the Vampire Slayer*, Buffy died how many times?

a. Twice b. Once

c. Four times d. Three times

809. What is Xena's horse's name?

a. Fargo b. Argo

c. Silver d. Ares

810. TRUE OR FALSE? THE TV SHOW *KRYPTON* WAS ORIGINALLY PLANNED AS BEING PART OF THE DC EXTENDED UNIVERSE.

MATCH THE FOLLOWING CHARACTERS TO THE TV SHOWS THEY APPEAR IN:

811. Willow Rosenberg   *a. Stranger Things*
812. Kara "Starbuck" Thrace   *b. Firefly*
813. Veronica Lodge   *c. Star Trek: Deep Space Nine*
814. Jim Hopper   *d. Buffy the Vampire Slayer*
815. Daisy Johnson   *e. Riverdale*
816. Emma Swan   *f. Marvel's Runaways*
817. Seven of Nine   *g. Agents of S.H.I.E.L.D.*
818. Hoban "Wash" Washburne   *h. Battlestar Galactica*
819. Nico Minoru   *i. Once Upon a Time*
820. Quark   *j. Star Trek: Voyager*

820. ON *THE 100*, WHAT IS THE FLAME?

821. True or false? Barry Allen derives his "Flash" powers from the Speed Force.

822. What is the name of the starship the Deep Space Nine station uses in battle?

a. USS *Defiant*   b. USS *Enterprise*   c. USS *Avenger*   d. USS *Defender*

823. Quark, the money-hungry bar owner on Deep Space Nine, is what kind of alien?

a. Jem'Hadar   b. Romulan

c. Borg   d. Ferengi

. . . .

824. Where is Xena's last battle?
a. Sparta
b. Mount Fuji
c. The shores of the Nile
d. Mount Olympus

. . . .

825. In *Buffy the Vampire Slayer,* what are the well-dressed demons who steal everyone's voices called?
a. The Gents
b. The Corporation
c. The Gentlemen
d. The Quartet

TOUGH TRIVIA CHALLENGE

826. On *Marvel's Runaways,* Molly has super strength, but has to do what after using it?
a. Bathe   b. Sing
c. Rest   d. Eat

827. TRUE OR FALSE? THE SECRETIVE GROUP ON GOTHAM IS KNOWN AS THE COURT OF OWLS.

. . . .

828. On the 1970s show *The Incredible Hulk,* what was the name of the man who became the Hulk?

. . . .

829. On *Cloak and Dagger,* what is the name of the company whose illegal activities gave Tandy and Tyrone their powers?

. . . .

830. True or false?
On *Star Trek: The Next Generation,* Captain Picard refers to Commander Riker as "Number Two."

. . . .

831. On *Star Trek: Voyager,* what is the Phage?

a. A flesh-rotting disease
b. A group time-traveling aliens
c. A computer program
d. A flu-like sickness

832. What is the name of the secret organization Supergirl works with?

   a. The DEO b. The CIA
   c. The FBI   d. The MIB

833. In Buffy *the Vampire Slayer*, what is Glory?

   a. A demon
   b. A god
   c. An angel
   d. A fairy

834. On *Xena*, Gabrielle has what weakness?

   a. She's afraid of the dark
   b. She gets seasick
   c. She's afraid of heights
   d. She gets headaches

835. In *Buffy the Vampire Slayer*, what is the name of the fearsome cyborg demon in season 4?

   a. Cain   b. Giles
   c. Eli   d. Adam

836. *On Riverdale*, what is the name of Jughead's younger sister?

837. True or false? In *Star Trek: Deep Space Nine*, the inhabitants of the wormhole are called the "the Seers" by the Bajorans.

838. True or false? On *Marvel's Runaways*, Karolina Dean is in love with Chase Stein.

839. *The Vampire Diaries* is set in which town?

840. What is interesting about Voyager's doctor?

   a. He's a child
   b. He's a hologram
   c. He's a robot
   d. He's a Klingon

841. Commander Data has a "twin" named what?
a. Process
b. Drive
c. Data 2
d. Lore

842. On *Marvel's Runaways*, what is unique about Karolina?
a. She's an Inhuman
b. She's a mutant
c. She's half-alien
d. She's a vampire

843. In *Buffy the Vampire Slayer*, what happens to Spike in season seven?
a. He gets sent back to England
b. He gets his soul back
c. He becomes human
d. He becomes a demon

844. In *Buffy the Vampire Slayer*, who has Buffy not had a romantic relationship with?
a. Angel   b. Xander
c. Riley   d. Spike

845. In Star *Trek: Voyager*, where in the galaxy is the ship stranded?
a. The Alpha Quadrant
b. The Beta Quadrant
c. The Delta Quadrant
d. The Gamma Quadrant

TOUGH TRIVIA CHALLENGE

846. True or false? On Buffy the Vampire Slayer, Dawn, Buffy's sister, is also known as the Key.

847. On *Angel*, Cordelia's demon contact is named what?

848. On *Star Trek: Voyager*, which aliens are so powerful that even the Borg fear them?
a. Species 1234   b. The Ocampa
c. The Dominion   d. Species 8472

849. In *Buffy the Vampire Slayer*, Willow and her girlfriend Tara are what?
a. Demons   b. Witches
c. Angels   d. Vampires

850. In *Buffy the Vampire Slayer*, Darla sired which important vampire?
a. Spike   b. Angel
c. The Master   d. Vlad

CLASSICAL, JAZZ & COUNTRY

851. In classical music, the seventeenth and eighteenth centuries are known as what period?

    a. Renaissance   b. Rococo

    c. Baroque   d. Classical

852. Though he lived much of his adult life in England, composer George Frideric Handel was born where?

    a. Germany   **b. France**

    c. Switzerland   **d. Austria**

853. Who wrote the orchestral jazz piece, "Rhapsody in Blue"?

    a. Duke Ellington

    b. Samuel Barber

    c. Benny Goodman

    d. George Gershwin

TOUGH TRIVIA CHALLENGE

854. True or false? Bluegrass music comes in part from Irish and Scottish folk music.

MATCH THE FOLLOWING COMPOSERS WITH THEIR NATIVE COUNTRIES:

855. Claude Debussy   a. Poland
856. Ralph Vaughan Williams   b. France
857. Aaron Copland   c. Bohemia (modern day Czech
858. Ludwig van Beethoven   Republic)
859. Frédéric Chopin   d. Austria
860. Wolfgang Amadeus Mozart   e. United States
861. Peter Tchaikovsky   f. Hungary
862. Antonio Vivaldi   g. England
863. Bela Bartok   h. Germany
864. Antonín Dvořák   i. Russia
     j. Italy

865. WHO WROTE AND SANG THE COUNTRY SONG "JOLENE"?

866. The Charlie Daniels Band released which song which was a mega hit?

a. "Demon on My Shoulder in Jacksonville"
b. "The Devil Went Down to Alabama"
c. "The Angels Went up to New York"
d. "The Devil Went Down to Georgia"

867. Which female vocalist sang "I'm a Little Bit Country" on her variety TV show?

a. Tammy Wynette
b. Marie Osmond
c. Carrie Underwood
d. June Carter Cash

868. Which American city is considered the birthplace of jazz?
   a. St. Louis   b. New York   c. New Orleans   d. Los Angeles

869. How many strings does a violin have?
a. Three   b. Four   c. Five   d. Six

870. Richard Strauss' piece, "Also Sprach Zarathustra" was used in which famous science fiction movie?
   a. *Star Wars*
   b. *Close Encounters of the Third Kind*
   c. *2001: A Space Odyssey*
   d. *ET*

871. How many keys does a full-size piano have?
   a. 74   b. 88   c. 96   d. 102

872. TRUE OR FALSE? THE COMPOSER JOHANN SEBASTIAN BACH HAD 20 CHILDREN.

873. What does "opus" mean in a composer's piece?

874. True or false? Holst wrote "The Planets" because of his interest in astrology.

♦ ♦ ♦ ♦ ♦ ♦ ♦ ♦ ♦ ♦ ♦ ♦ ♦ ♦ ♦

875. How many instrument sections are there in a modern orchestra?

a. Three   b. Four

c. Five   d. Six

♦ ♦ ♦ ♦ ♦ ♦ ♦ ♦ ♦ ♦ ♦ ♦ ♦ ♦ ♦

876. Mozart was a young man when he died. How old was he?

a. 25
b. 30
c. 35
d. 21

877. "Ride of the Valkyries" is from an opera by which composer?

a. Giacomo Puccini
b. Richard Strauss
c. Hector Berlioz
d. Richard Wagner

878. What was the nickname of the famed jazz trumpeter and singer, Louis Armstrong?

a. The Prince
b. Duke
c. Satchmo
d. Smooth

♦ ♦ ♦ ♦ ♦ ♦ ♦ ♦ ♦ ♦ ♦ ♦ ♦ ♦ ♦

879. "I Walk the Line" is a number one country hit by which artist?

a. Roy Clark
b. Buck Owens
c. Johnny Cash
d. Hank Williams

♦ ♦ ♦ ♦ ♦ ♦ ♦ ♦ ♦ ♦ ♦ ♦ ♦ ♦ ♦

880. What is a honky-tonk?

a. A delivery truck
b. An old car
c. A concert hall
d. A kind of bar

♦ ♦ ♦ ♦ ♦ ♦ ♦ ♦ ♦ ♦ ♦ ♦ ♦ ♦ ♦

881. True or false? Swing jazz was a new style that came after Bebop jazz.

♦ ♦ ♦ ♦ ♦ ♦ ♦ ♦ ♦ ♦ ♦ ♦ ♦ ♦ ♦

882. What instruments make up a string quartet?

MATCH THE FOLLOWING JAZZ MUSICIANS WITH THEIR INSTRUMENTS:

883. Miles Davis	**a. Clarinet**
884. Bill Evans	**b. Drums**
885. John Coltrane	**c. Violin**
886. Billie Holiday	**d. Guitar**
887. Buddy Rich	**e. Saxophone**
888. Pat Metheny	**f. Vibraphone**
889. Lionel Hampton	**g. Trombone**
890. Benny Goodman	**h. Piano**
891. Glenn Miller	**i. Voice**
892. Stéphane Grappelli	**j. Trumpet**

893. WHAT INSTRUMENTS MOST OFTEN MAKE UP THE CLASSIC JAZZ TRIO?

894. Swing was the most popular kind of jazz during what time?

a. 1930s—40s

b. 1940s—50s

c. 1950s—60s

d. 1960s—70s

TOUGH TRIVIA CHALLENGE

895. The large, tuned kettle drums in an orchestra are called what?
a. Snares
b. Timpani
c. Toms
d. Bass drums

896. The keyboard instrument that was most popular in classical music before the piano was which of these?

a. Monochord   b. Clavichord   c. Autochord   d. Harpsichord

897. What was the name of the night club in Harlem where the Duke Ellington Orchestra played?

898. In 1959, Miles Davis released what many consider the greatest jazz album ever. What is it called?

a. *Back in Black*
b. *Pretty in Pink*
c. *Deep Purple*
d. *Kind of Blue*

899. What is Tchaikovsky's most famous ballet?

a. Cinderella
b. The Rite of Spring
c. The Nutcracker
d. Giselle

900. TRUE OR FALSE? RAGTIME WAS EARLY TWENTIETH-CENTURY STYLE OF MUSIC THAT INFLUENCED JAZZ.

POPULAR

901. *Tommy* is a rock opera by which English band?

a. The Who
b. Cream
c. The Yardbirds
d. Deep Purple

902. Which band did vocalist Sting used to sing for?

a. The Ramones
b. U2
c. The Police
d. Dire Straits

903. The Southern rock band Lynyrd Skynyrd had a concert favorite with which song?
   a. "Smoke on the Water"
   b. "Free Bird"
   c. "Ramblin' Man"
   d. "Hotel California"

904. TRUE OR FALSE? MADONNA WAS ORIGINALLY A MEMBER OF THE RUNAWAYS.

905. Who sang the words, "Excuse me while I kiss the sky"?
   a. John Lennon   b. Jim Morrison
   c. Janis Joplin   d. Jimi Hendrix

MATCH THE FOLLOWING BANDS OR SINGERS TO THEIR COUNTRIES OF ORIGIN:

906. Keith Urban   a. Canada
907. Kylie Minogue   b. Barbados
908. Celine Dion   c. Germany
909. The Who   d. Trinidad and Tobago
910. Rihanna   e. New Zealand
911. The Corrs   f. Australia
912. Bjork   g. England
913. The Scorpions   h. Ireland
914. Shakira   i. Colombia
915. Nicki Minaj   j. Iceland

Answers: 896. d; 897. The Cotton Club; 898. d; 899. c; 900. True; 901. a; 902. c; 903. b; 904. False, she was a member of Breakfast Club and Emmy; 905. d; 906. e; 907. f; 908. a; 909. g; 910. b; 911. h; 912. j; 913. c; 914. i; 915. d

Culture & Entertainment • 105

916. WHAT IS THE STAGE NAME OF SINGER ROBYN FENTY?

▲ ▲ ▲ ▲ ▲ ▲ ▲ ▲ ▲ ▲ ▲ ▲ ▲ ▲ ▲

917. Michael Lee Aday has what better-known stage name?
- a. Prime Rib
- b. Sirloin
- c. Chuck Burger
- d. Meatloaf

▲ ▲ ▲ ▲ ▲ ▲ ▲ ▲ ▲ ▲ ▲ ▲ ▲ ▲

918. Micky Dolenz was a member of what animal-named band?
- a. The Ants
- b. The Mosquitos
- c. The Beatles
- d. The Monkees

▲ ▲ ▲ ▲ ▲ ▲ ▲ ▲ ▲ ▲ ▲ ▲ ▲ ▲

919. "Rock Around the Clock" was a hit song for who?
- a. Bill Haley and the Planets
- b. Jack Haley and the Asteroids
- c. Bill Haley and the Comets
- d. Will Haley and the Meteors

920. Who released the album *Appetite for Destruction*?
- a. Guns N' Roses
- b. Poison
- c. Ratt
- d. Motley Crue

▲ ▲ ▲ ▲ ▲ ▲ ▲ ▲ ▲ ▲ ▲ ▲ ▲ ▲ ▲

921. Elvis Presley served in which branch of the armed forces?
- a. Army
- b. Navy
- c. Air Force
- d. Marines

▲ ▲ ▲ ▲ ▲ ▲ ▲ ▲ ▲ ▲ ▲ ▲

922. After leaving Deep Purple, guitarist Ritchie Blackmore formed which band?
- a. Renaissance
- b. Elf
- c. Rainbow
- d. Dio

923. One of the first rap hits was called "Rapper's Delight." Who recorded it?

   a. Public Enemy
   b. N.W.A.
   c. The Sugar Hill Gang
   d. Run-D.M.C.

▲▲▲▲▲▲▲▲▲▲▲▲▲

924. Who was the first woman singer to be inducted into the Rock and Roll Hall of Fame?

   a. Aretha Franklin
   b. Whitney Houston
   c. Janis Joplin
   d. Diana Ross

▲▲▲▲▲▲▲▲▲▲▲▲▲▲

925. What was the name of the Beatles' record label?

   a. Blackberry
   b. Apple
   c. Pear
   d. Pineapple

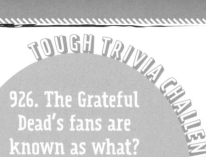

TOUGH TRIVIA CHALLENGE

926. The Grateful Dead's fans are known as what?
   a. The Folks
   b. Deadies
   c. Deadheads
   d. The Grateful Ones

927. Which band released an album called "Dark Side of the Moon"?

   a. Soylent Green
   b. Pink Floyd
   c. Deep Purple
   d. Deep Sea Blue

▲▲▲▲▲▲▲▲▲▲▲▲▲▲

928. Journey calls which city home?
   a. Los Angeles
   b. San Francisco
   c. Seattle
   d. Portland

Answers: 916. Rihanna; 917. d; 918. d; 919. c; 920. a; 921. a; 922. b; 923. c; 924. a; 925. b; 926. c; 927. b; 928. b.

Culture & Entertainment • **107**

929. The rock band Rush is from which country?
   a. United States
   b. Canada
   c. Great Britain
   d. France

930. Complete the Cyndi Lauper song title: "Girls Just Want to . . ."
   a. dance all night
   b. go out
   c. be cool
   d. have fun

931. Who wrote the rock anthem "Rock and Roll All Nite"?
   a. Blur
   b. Bad Company
   c. Thin Lizzy
   d. Kiss

932. Which singer was a member of the Mickey Mouse Club?
   a. Gwen Stefani
   b. Britney Spears
   c. Katy Perry
   d. Taylor Swift

933. "Gangnam Style" is performed by Psy, who is from which country?
   a. China
   b. Vietnam
   c. South Korea
   d. Japan

934. Which rapper is also known as "Slim Shady"?
   a. Jay-Z   b. LL Cool J
   c. Eminem   d. 50 Cent

935. According to Lorde, we'll never be what?
   a. Spoiled
   b. Royals
   c. Coiled
   d. Lawyers

936. TRUE OR FALSE? LL COOL J STANDS FOR "LIVIN' LARGE COOL JAMES."

MATCH THE FOLLOWING BANDS OR SINGERS WITH THEIR ALBUMS:

938. Taylor Swift	a. *Lemonade*
939. The Beatles	b. *Rumors*
940. Beyoncé	c. *Like a Prayer*
941. U2	d. *Anti*
942. The Rolling Stones	e. *Revolver*
943. Kansas	f. *Graceland*
944. Adele	g. *The Fame*
945. Fleetwood Mac	h. *Lateralus*
946. Tool	i. *The Joshua Tree*
947. Billy Joel	j. *thank u, next*
948. Justin Bieber	k. *Moving Pictures*
949. Madonna	l. *Purpose*
950. Lady Gaga	m. *1989*
951. Drake	n. *Tattoo You*
952. Rihanna	o. *Views*
953. Ariana Grande	p. *Master of Puppets*
954. Radiohead	q. *19*
955. Metallica	r. *OK Computer*
956. Rush	s. *Leftoverture*
957. Paul Simon	t. *The Stranger*

958. True or false? Despite their popularity, the Beatles never had a number one single.

Answers: 929. b; 930. d; 931. d; 932. b; 933. c; 934. c; 935. b; 936. False, it stands for "Ladies Love Cool James"; 937. Heart; 938. m; 939. e; 940. a; 941. i; 942. n; 943. s; 944. q; 945. b; 946. h; 947. t; 948. l; 949. c; 950. g; 951. o; 952. d; 953. j; 954. r; 955. p; 956. k; 957. f; 958. False, they had 17 number one singles.

Culture & Entertainment • 109

959. "Stairway to Heaven" is the most famous song by which band?
   a. Jethro Tull
   b. Kansas
   c. Led Zeppelin
   d. The Rolling Stones

960. Which band performed their last full live concert in 1966?
   a. The Beach Boys
   b. The Beatles
   c. The Rolling Stones
   d. The Doors

961. The Fender Stratocaster is what kind of instrument?
   a. Saxophone   b. Guitar
   c. Drum set   d. Bass

962. AC/DC comes from which country?
   a. Great Britain
   b. Australia
   c. Canada
   d. United States

963. One of Queen's most famous and best-loved songs is which of these?
   a. "Go Your Own Way"
   b. "Let It Be"
   c. "Bohemian Rhapsody"
   d. "I Will Survive"

964. Ozzy Osbourne has been the lead singer of which band more than once?
   a. Pink Floyd
   b. Iron Maiden
   c. Black Sabbath
   d. Judas Priest

965. According to Prince, we should "Party Like It's . . ."
   a. 1999   b. 2000
   c. 1989   d. 2009

966. WHAT IS LADY GAGA'S FAMOUS CATCHPHRASE?

967. True or false? Miley Cyrus is the younger sister of country singer Billy Ray Cyrus.

MATCH THE FOLLOWING SINGERS WITH THEIR BANDS:

968. Susanna Hoffs
969. Debbie Harry
970. Chris Martin
971. Stevie Nicks
972. Smokey Robinson
973. Liam Gallagher
974. Gwen Stefani
975. Phil Collins
976. James Hetfield
977. Billie Joe Armstrong

a. Oasis
b. Fleetwood Mac
c. The Bangles
d. Green Day
e. Genesis
f. Blondie
g. No Doubt
h. Metallica
i. Coldplay
j. The Miracles

978. TRUE OR FALSE? ARIANA GRANDE MADE HER BROADWAY DEBUT IN *13*.

979. "I Heard it Through the Grapevine" was a huge hit for who in 1968?

980. True or false? The Beatles' Paul McCartney is left-handed.

981. Sean Combs is better known by which stage name?
a. Puff Daddy   b. P. Diddy   c. Diddy   d. All of the above

982. Who wrote the 1960s classic song, "Born to Be Wild"?
- a. Steppenwolf
- b. The Who
- c. The Doors
- d. Jimi Hendrix

983. TRUE OR FALSE? SNOOP DOG WAS AN IMPORTANT PART OF THE WEST COAST HIP-HOP SCENE IN ITS EARLY DAYS.

984. ABBA comes from which European country?
- a. Norway
- b. Sweden
- c. Denmark
- d. Iceland

985. True or false? Jethro Tull is the name of that band's lead singer.

986. Actor Will Smith was originally in which rap group?
- a. DJ Jazzy Jeff & The Fresh Prince
- b. The Sugar Hill Gang
- c. 2 Live Crew
- d. Kid 'n Play

987. What was the name of Jay-Z's debut album?

988. TRUE OR FALSE? THE BAND KANSAS IS NOT ACTUALLY FROM KANSAS.

989. Who write the classic song, "Roll Over, Beethoven," and was known for his unusual skipping across the stage with his guitar?
- a. Elvis Presley
- b. Frankie Valli
- c. Chuck Berry
- d. Buddy Holly

990. Eddie and Alex are brothers in which band?
- a. UFO
- b. AC/DC
- c. Van Halen
- d. Quiet Riot

991. Who replaced David Lee Roth as lead singer in Van Halen in 1985?

992. The Beastie Boys hit debut 1986 album was called what?

a. *Paul's Boutique*
b. *Ill Communication*
c. *Check Your Head*
d. *Licensed to Ill*

993. True or false? Ian Gillan sang for both Deep Purple and Black Sabbath.

994. Shakira says which part doesn't lie?

a. Hands
b. Hips
c. Arms
d. Eyes

995. Which English band had a hit with the song "Roundabout" in 1972?

a. Camel
b. Yes
c. Genesis
d. Jethro Tull

996. WHO WAS THE FIRST FEMALE GROUP TO SIGN WITH MOTOWN RECORDS?

997. Actor Donald Glover has performed music under what name?

998. Gordon Sumner is better known by what stage name?

999. Before he was a solo artist, Peter Gabriel sang for which band?

a. Yes
b. Genesis
c. King Crimson
d. Gentle Giant

1,000. WHAT WAS THE FIRST TELEVISION SHOW THAT SELENA GOMEZ WAS IN?

ART & ART HISTORY

1,001. Where is the famous prehistoric art of southern France mainly located?
- a. On petrified wood
- b. On cave walls
- c. On the sides of cliffs
- d. On rocky outcroppings at cliff edges

1,002. Who is the Greek god of sculpture?
- a. Apollo
- b. Dionysus
- c. Ares
- d. Hephaestus

1,003. What is the name of the beautiful Irish or British gospel book from c. 800, now held by Trinity College in Dublin, Ireland?
- a. The Book of Calls
- b. The Lindisfarne Gospels
- c. The Book of Kells
- d. The Mabinogion

1,004. Leonardo da Vinci's *Mona Lisa* is probably a portrait of who?
- a. Lisa Minelli
- b. His wife
- c. Himself as a woman
- d. Lisa Gherardini

1,005. TRUE OR FALSE? IN THE LATE EIGHTEENTH CENTURY, EUROPE WAS DOMINATED BY THE NEOCLASSICAL STYLE.

1,006. Which famous French art gallery has a large glass pyramid outside?

1,007. What painting style wanted to show everything about a subject, good and bad?

    a. Harshness   b. Surrealism   c. Realism   d. Classicism

1,008. After an argument with Gauguin, Van Gogh did what?

    a. Cut off the tip of his little finger   b. Jumped in a river to drown himself

    c. Cut off part of his own left ear   d. Punched his fist through a door

1,009. True or false? A large number of medieval Eruopean artists are anonymous, since it was believed that one's work was for the glory of God and not oneself.

1,010. Salvador Dali's painting style is most often called what?

    a. Dadaism   b. Surrealism
    c. Impressionism   d. Cubism

1,011. Which architect redesigned St. Paul's Cathedral after the medieval original was destroyed in the London fire of 1666?

    a. Inigo Jones   b. Ben Jonson
    c. Nicholas Hawksmoor   d. Christopher Wren

MATCH THE ARTWORKS TO THEIR ARTISTS:

1,012. *The Birth of Venus*

1,013. *Café Terrace at Night*

1,014. *The Creation of Adam*

1,015. *American Gothic*

1,016. *Mona Lisa*

1,017. *The Garden of Earthly Delights*

1,018. *The Persistence of Memory*

1,019. *The Thinker*

1,020. *The Ambassadors*

1,021. *The Kiss*

a. Vincent van Gogh

b. Gustav Klimt

c. Leonardo da Vinci

d. Michelangelo

e. Hans Holbein the Younger

f. Grant Wood

g. Auguste Rodin

h. Hieronymus Bosch

i. Salvador Dali

j. Botticelli

1,022. WHICH LATE NINETEENTH-CENTURY STYLE EMPHASIZED NATURAL SHAPES AND CURVES, ESPECIALLY THOSE IN FLOWERS AND PLANTS?

▲▲▲▲▲▲▲▲▲▲▲▲▲▲▲▲▲▲▲▲▲▲▲▲▲▲

1,023. Which group of nineteenth-century artists returned to early Renaissance styles and often painted mythic or religious subjects?

a. Impressionists   b. Realists

c. Pre-Raphaelites   d. Romantics

▲▲▲▲▲▲▲▲▲▲▲▲▲▲▲▲▲▲▲▲▲▲▲▲▲▲

1,024. What was the name of the art style that dominated Europe in the early eighteenth century?
 a. Neo-Classical
 b. Baroque
 c. Renaissance
 d. Rococo

1,025. True or false? Frida Kahlo was a Mexican artist who painted mostly self-portraits.

1,026. Who drew a picture of a rhinoceros even though he'd never seen one?
 a. Hans Holbein
 b. Albrecht Durer
 c. Michelangelo
 d. Leonardo da Vinci

1,027. Which Dutch artist created pictures of optical illusions?
 a. Van Gogh
 b. Rubens
 c. M. C. Escher
 d. Rembrandt

1,028. TRUE OR FALSE? LEONARD DA VINCI PAINTED THE SISTINE CHAPEL.

1,029. THE IDEA OF THE HIERATIC SCALE IN ART USES WHAT TO DETERMINE THE IMPORTANCE OF AN OBJECT OR FIGURE?

1,030. *Water Lilies* is a series of paintings by which Impressionist?
 a. Gauguin
 b. Monet
 c. Matisse
 d. Manet

1,031. Which of these artists is best known for a painting of his mother?
a. Leonardo da Vinci
b. James Abbott McNeill Whistler
c. Vincent Van Gogh
d. Auguste Rodin

◆ ◆ ◆ ◆ ◆ ◆ ◆ ◆ ◆ ◆ ◆ ◆ ◆ ◆ ◆

1,032. The ancient Greek Elgin Marbles are held in which museum?

1,033. Jackson Pollock's artistic style is known as which of these?
a. Abstract Expressionism
b. Realism
c. Cubism
d. Neo-Gothic

1,034. Van Gogh's *The Starry Night* shows which southern French town?
a. Avignon
b. Saint-Rémy-de-Provence
c. Arles
d. Aix-en-Provence

1,035. What is chiaroscuro in painting?
a. The use of pastel colors for a muted effect
b. A type of paint made from egg whites
c. The use of contrast between light and dark
d. A special type of paint brush for details

◆ ◆ ◆ ◆ ◆ ◆ ◆ ◆ ◆ ◆ ◆ ◆ ◆ ◆ ◆

1,036. True or false? Picasso was devoted to detailed realism throughout his life.

◆ ◆ ◆ ◆ ◆ ◆ ◆ ◆ ◆ ◆ ◆ ◆ ◆ ◆ ◆

1,037. Which movement called itself "anti-art"?

◆ ◆ ◆ ◆ ◆ ◆ ◆ ◆ ◆ ◆ ◆ ◆ ◆ ◆ ◆

1,038. Which artistic style revolted against Enlightenment and overly scientific thinking?
a. Impressionism
b. Cubism
c. Rococo
d. Romanticism

1,039. NICHOLAS HILLIARD WAS AN ENGLISH RENAISSANCE PAINTER WITH WHICH SPECIALTY?

A. MINIATURE PORTRAITS   B. LANDSCAPES

C. MURALS   D. ENGRAVINGS

1,040. Leonardo da Vinci's mural *The Last Supper* originally also showed what, which was accidentally removed in the seventeenth century?

a. Matthew's right arm   b. Judas's hands

c. Peter's left hand   d. Jesus's feet

MATCH EACH FOLLOWING ARTIST WITH THEIR NATIVE COUNTRY:

1,041. John Butler Yeats   a. England
1,042. Leonardo da Vinci   b. Ireland
1,043. Peter Paul Rubens   c. The Netherlands
1,044. Henri Matisse   d. Spain
1,045. Andy Warhol   e. Italy
1,046. Paul Klee   f. Switerland
1,047. John Constable   g. Germany/Belgium
1,048. Hieronymus Bosch   h. Greece
1,049. Polygnotus   i. France
1,050. Pablo Picasso   j. United States

CHAPTER 3

Geopgraphy & Earth Science

WORLD GEOGRAPHY

1,051. Which of these is the world's largest desert?
a. Kalahari
b. Mojave
c. Gobi
d. Sahara

1,052. Which stretch of water separates Spain and Morocco?
a. The Bering Strait
b. The Barbary Coast
c. The Strait of Gibraltar
d. The Aegean Sea

1,053. What is the name of Japan's main island?
a. Nihon
b. Japan
c. Honshu
d. Nippon

1,054. Mount Kilimanjaro is located in which country?
a. Kenya
b. Tanzania
c. Congo
d. Mozambique

1,055. Which of these is a part of the United Kingdom?
a. Guernsey
b. Northern Ireland
c. Faroe Islands
d. Jersey

1,056. Which is the largest country on the Arabian Peninsula?
a. Oman
b. Yemen
c. Saudi Arabia
d. Egypt

Answers: 1,051. d; 1,052. c; 1,053. c; 1,054. b; 1,055. b; 1,056. c

1,057. TRUE OR FALSE? CANADA HAS OVER HALF OF THE NATURAL LAKES IN THE WORLD.

MATCH THE FOLLOWING EUROPEAN COUNTRIES WITH THEIR CAPITALS:

1,058. France	a. Ljubljana
1,059. Germany	b. Helsinki
1,060. Italy	c. Paris
1,061. United Kingdom	d. Zagreb
1,062. Bulgaria	e. Rome
1,063. Slovenia	f. Sofia
1,064. Latvia	g. Warsaw
1,065. Poland	h. Berlin
1,066. Finland	i. London
1,067. Croatia	j. Riga

1,068. WHAT COUNTRY BORDERS SWITZERLAND TO THE SOUTH?

1,069. True or false? There is a bridge that links Europe to Asia.

1,070. What is Eyjafjallajökull?

a. A Danish coastline   b. A fjord in Norway

c. An island near Sweden   d. A volcano in Iceland

1,071. Which country makes up most of Central America?

   a. Nicaragua
   b. El Salvador
   c. Mexico
   d. Honduras

▲▲▲▲▲▲▲▲▲▲▲▲▲▲

1,072. Which country has the largest number of volcanoes?

   a. New Zealand
   b. Australia
   c. Indonesia
   d. India

▲▲▲▲▲▲▲▲▲▲▲▲▲▲

1,073. The Black Forest is located in which European country?

   a. Scotland
   b. Germany
   c. Switzerland
   d. Romania

▲▲▲▲▲▲▲▲▲▲▲▲▲▲

1,074. Which mountain range forms the traditional boundary between Europe and Asia?

   a. The Urals
   b. The Alps
   c. The Andes
   d. The Pennines

▲▲▲▲▲▲▲▲▲▲▲▲▲▲

1,075. Which is the tallest mountain in the Alps?

   a. Dom
   b. Mont Blanc
   c. Weisshorn
   d. The Matterhorn

TOUGH TRIVIA CHALLENGE

1,076. TRUE OR FALSE? NO NATION OWNS ANTARCTICA.

1,077. What is the only city that is in both Europe and Asia?

◆◆◆◆◆◆◆◆◆◆◆◆◆◆◆◆◆◆◆◆◆◆◆◆◆◆◆◆◆◆◆◆◆◆◆◆◆◆

1,078. The southernmost tip of Africa is known as:
    a. The Cape of Good Hope   b. Cape Horn
    c. Cape Cod   d. Cape Agulhas

◆◆◆◆◆◆◆◆◆◆◆◆◆◆◆◆◆◆◆◆◆◆◆◆◆◆◆◆◆◆◆◆◆◆◆◆◆◆

1,079. What is the name for the area of water that divides the northern and southern islands of New Zealand?
    a. The Dire Strait   **b. The Cook Strait**
    c. The Bering Strait   **d. The Strait of Magellan**

◆◆◆◆◆◆◆◆◆◆◆◆◆◆◆◆◆◆◆◆◆◆◆◆◆◆◆◆◆◆◆◆◆◆◆◆◆◆

1,080. Which city has the largest population?
    a. Tokyo   b. Shanghai
    c. Mexico City   d. Beijing

1,081. What artificial construction connects the Atlantic Ocean to the Pacic Ocean?

1,082. The Atlas Mountains are located in which area?
    a. South America   b. South Africa
    c. North Africa   d. Greece and Macedonia

◆◆◆◆◆◆◆◆◆◆◆◆◆◆◆◆◆◆◆◆◆◆◆◆◆◆◆◆◆◆◆◆◆◆◆◆◆◆

1,083. Which is the world's longest river?
a. The Nile   b. The Amazon   c. The Congo   d. The Mississippi

MATCH THE FOLLOWING ASIAN COUNTRIES WITH THEIR CAPITALS:

1,084. China
1,085. Japan
1,086. Laos
1,087. Armenia
1,088. Myanmar (Burma)
1,089. Afghanistan
1,090. Kazakhstan
1,091. Georgia
1,092. Tajikistan
1,093. Vietnam
1,094. South Korea
1,095. Malaysia
1,096. Nepal
1,097. Cambodia
1,098. Jordan

a. Seoul
b. Amman
c. Yerevan
d. Tokyo
e. Kabul
f. Beijing
g. Vientiane
h. Phnom Penh
i. Dushanbe
j. Kuala Lumpur
k. Nur-Sultan
l. Hanoi
m. Kathmandu
n. Tbilisi
o. Naypyidaw

1,099. TRUE OR FALSE? GREENLAND IS THE LARGEST ISLAND IN THE WORLD.

1,100. What does "Uluru" in central Australia translate as?

a. Great Pebble   b. Little Rock

c. Great Rock   d. The Stone

1,101. How many time zones does Canada have?

a. Two   b. Four   c. Five   d. Six

Answers: 1,077. Istanbul; 1,078. d; 1,079. b; 1,080. d; 1,081. The Panama Canal; 1,082. c; 1,083. a; 1,084. f; 1,085. d; 1,086. g; 1,087. c; 1,088. o; 1,089. e; 1,090. k; 1,091. n; 1,092. i; 1,093. l; 1,094. a; 1,095. j; 1,096. m; 1,097. h; 1,098. b; 1,099. True; 1,100. a; 1,101. d

Geography & Earth Science • 125

1,102. True or false? Morocco is one of only three countries (along with Spain and France) that has coasts on both the Atlantic Ocean and Mediterranean Sea.

1,103. Which continent has the most countries?
  a. Asia
  b. Africa
  c. South America
  d. North America

1,104. Which of these is the world's smallest independent nation?
  a. Liechtenstein
  b. Andorra
  c. Monaco
  d. Vatican City

1,105. The Great Barrier Reef is located near which country?
  a. China   b. New Zealand
  c. Indonesia   d. Australia

1,106. WHICH IS THE LARGEST SCANDINAVIAN COUNTRY?

1,107. Which is the largest lake in Africa?

1,108. The Gobi desert is located on which continent?
  a. North America b. Asia
  c. Africa   d. Antarctica

1,109. True or false? **Africa is the only continent that is in all four of the world's hemispheres: Northern, Southern, Eastern, and Western**

1,110. NAME THE WORLD'S FIVE OCEANS.

1,111. Which mountain range is the longest in the world?
**a. The Rockies b. The Himalayas
c. The Urals   d. The Andes**

1,112. About what percentage of the world's people live in Asia?

    a. 70
    b. 45
    c. 50
    d. 60

TOUGH TRIVIA CHALLENGE

1,113. Australia is situated between which two oceans?

MATCH THE FOLLOWING AFRICAN COUNTRIES WITH THEIR CAPITALS:

1,114. Egypt	a. Rabat
1,115. Tanzania	b. Cairo
1,116. Ethiopia	c. Banjul
1,117. Angola	d. Nairobi
1,118. Ghana	e. Addis Ababa
1,119. Morocco	f. Dodoma
1,120. Nigeria	g. Abuja
1,121. Kenya	h. Luanda
1,122. Mozambique	i. Maputo
1,123. Senegal	j. Dakar
1,124. Rwanda	k. Kigali
1,125. Gambia	l. N'Djamena
1,126. Chad	m. Accra
1,127. Libya	n. Tripoli
1,128. Botswana	o. Gaborone

Answers: 1,102.True; 1,103. b; 1,104. d; 1,105. d; 1,106. Sweden; 1,107. Lake Victoria; 1,108. b; 1,109.True; 1,110. Arctic Ocean, Atlantic Ocean, Indian Ocean, Pacific Ocean, and Southern Ocean; 1,111. d; 1,112. d; 1,113. Indian and Pacific; 1,114. b; 1,115. f; 1,116. e; 1,117. h; 1,118. m; 1,119. a; 1,120. g; 1,121. d; 1,122. i; 1,123. j; 1,124. k; 1,125. c; 1,126. l; 1,127. n; 1,128. o.

Geography & Earth Science • **127**

1,129. TRUE OR FALSE? ANTARCTICA IS THE DRIEST PLACE ON EARTH.

1,130. Which is the world's largest sea?

a. Red Sea

b. Caspian Sea

c. Black Sea

d. Mediterranean Sea

1,131. Antarctica contains about what percentage of the world's fresh water?

a. 75   b. 90

c. 80   d. 50

1,132. Which ocean increases in size by an inch or so every year?

1,133. True or false? Africa is the world's largest continent.

1,134. Which country has the most pyramids?

a. Sudan

b. Egypt

c. Libya

d. Somalia

1,135. Which country entirely surrounds Lesotho?

a. Algeria

b. South Africa

c. Angola

d. Namibia

1,136. WHAT IS THE ONLY COUNTRY THAT PORTUGAL BORDERS?

1,137. Which city is probably the oldest in the world?

a. Kabul   b. Damascus

c. Beijing   d. Baghdad

1,138. True or false? The United States and Canada share the longest international border.

1,139. What is the southernmost capital city in the world?

1,140. True or false? Amman, the capital of Jordan, used to be called Philadelphia.

MATCH THE FOLLOWING SOUTH AMERICAN COUNTRIES WITH THEIR CAPITALS:

1,141. Argentina	a. Caracas
1,142. Peru	b. Bogotá
1,143. Brazil	c. Paramaribo
1,144. Venezuela	d. Buenos Aires
1,145. Chile	e. Lima
1,146. Colombia	f. Quito
1,147. Ecuador	g. Asunción
1,148. Uruguay	h. Brasilia
1,149. Paraguay	i. Santiago
1,150. Suriname	j. Montevideo

•U.S. GEOGRAPHY•

1,151. What is the longest river in the United States?
a. Missouri
b. Colorado
c. Mississippi
d. Rio Grande

1,152. In which state is Mount Rushmore?
a. Utah
b. South Dakota
c. Wyoming
d. North Dakota

TOUGH TRIVIA CHALLENGE

1,153. Which river flows through the Grand Canyon?
a. Rio Grande
b. Missouri
c. Mississippi
d. Colorado

1,154. What is the largest national park in the United States?
a. Wrangell-St. Elias, in Alaska
b. Zion, in Utah
c. Yellowstone, in Wyoming, Idaho, and Montana
d. Grand Teton, in Wyoming

1,155. NORTH CAROLINA AND SOUTH CAROLINA WERE NAMED AFTER WHICH KING?

1,156. Which U.S. city has a part of Canada south of it?
a. Buffalo
b. Detroit
c. Duluth
d. Lake Geneva

1,157. Where is Mount St. Helens?

a. Oregon   b. California

c. Washington   d. Idaho

1,158. Which state has the longest coastline?

a. California   b. Alaska

c. Florida   d. Texas

1,159. TRUE OR FALSE? DENALI IS THE TALLEST MOUNTAIN IN THE U.S.

MATCH EACH STATE TO ITS CAPITAL:

1,160. Nevada	a. Carson City
1,161. California	b. Montpelier
1,162. Oregon	c. Lincoln
1,163. Colorado	d. Denver
1,164. Mississippi	e. Augusta
1,165. South Carolina	f. Columbia
1,166. Kentucky	g. Sacramento
1,167. Vermont	h. Little Rock
1,168. Florida	i. Columbus
1,169. Arkansas	j. Salem
1,170. Illinois	k. Tallahassee
1,171. North Dakota	l. Bismarck
1,172. Ohio	m. Jackson
1,173. Nebraska	n. Frankfort
1,174. Maine	o. Springfield

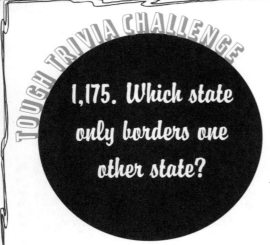

1,175. Which state only borders one other state?

1,176. How many states contain a part of the Mojave Desert?

  a. Three   b. One

  c. Four   d. Two

1,177. Which U.S. city is known as "The Windy City"?

  a. Chicago
  b. Cleveland
  c. New York
  d. Buffalo

▲▲▲▲▲▲▲▲▲▲▲▲▲

1,178. Which U.S. city is home to the Space Needle?

  a. Portland
  b. Vancouver
  c. Seattle
  d. Bellingham

▲▲▲▲▲▲▲▲▲▲▲▲▲▲▲▲▲▲▲▲▲▲▲

1,179. The mountain called Mauna Kea is in which state?

  a. Alaska b. Washington c. Hawaii d. Colorado

▲▲▲▲▲▲▲▲▲▲▲▲▲▲▲▲▲▲▲▲▲▲▲▲▲

1,180. TRUE OR FALSE? RHODE ISLAND IS THE SMALLEST STATE IN THE U.S.

▲▲▲▲▲▲▲▲▲▲▲▲▲▲▲▲▲▲▲▲▲▲▲▲▲

MATCH EACH STATE WITH ITS MOTTO:

▲▲▲▲▲▲▲▲▲▲▲▲▲▲▲▲▲▲▲▲▲▲▲▲

1,181. Utah

1,182. Texas

1,183. New York

1,184. Louisiana

1,185. Indiana

1,186. Alaska

1,187. New Jersey

1,188. Nebraska

1,189. Wyoming

1,190. New Hampshire

a. Friendship

b. Equal rights

c. Excelsior!

d. Industry

e. Liberty and prosperity

f. North to the future

g. Live free or die

h. Union, justice, and confidence

i. The crossroads of America

j. Equality before the law

▲▲▲▲▲▲▲▲▲▲▲▲▲▲▲▲▲▲▲▲▲▲▲▲▲▲▲▲▲▲

1,191. What area is the lowest point in the U.S.?

1,192. At which city do the Mississippi and the Missouri Rivers meet?
- a. Kansas City
- b. St. Louis
- c. Little Rock
- d. Jacksonville

1,193. Alaska was bought from which country?
a. Russia   b. Canada   c. Japan   d. China

1,194. WHICH STATE IS KNOWN AS "THE GARDEN STATE"?

◆ ◆

1,195. True or false? Lake Michigan is the only Great Lake located completely within the U.S. border.

◆ ◆

1,196. TRUE OR FALSE? PUERTO RICO IS A STATE.

◆ ◆ ◆ ◆ ◆ ◆ ◆ ◆ ◆ ◆ ◆ ◆ ◆

TOUGH TRIVIA CHALLENGE

1,198. Which of these is the longest Interstate Highway in the U.S.?
a. I-5   b. I-90
c. Route 66   d. I-80

1,197. Which is the only state located partly in the Eastern Hemisphere?
a. Guam   b. Maine
c. Alaska   d. Hawaii

◆ ◆

1,199. True or false? Iowa borders one of the Great Lakes

◆ ◆

1,200. What is the name of the famous geyser at Yellowstone National Park?

1,201. What is the molten rock below the earth's surface is called?
  a. Lava
  b. Magma
  c. Liquid rock
  d. Earth water

1,202. Which of these formations shows how a glacier flowed?
  a. Crevasse
  b. Cirque
  c. Drumlin
  d. Meander

1,203. What geological process describes how the Grand Canyon was formed?
  a. Withering
  b. Erosion
  c. Weathering
  d. Decay

1,204. True or false? "Petrichor" means the nice smell of the rain after a dry period.

MATCH THE WORLD'S FIVE TALLEST MOUNTAINS TO THEIR SIZES, FROM TALLEST (FIRST) TO LEAST TALL (FIFTH):

1,205. Lhotse
1,206. K2
1,207. Makalu
1,208. Everest
1,209. Kangchenjunga

a. Fourth
b. First
c. Fifth
d. Third
e. Second

1,210. A STRONG WIND THAT BLOWS THROUGH SOUTHERN FRANCE IS KNOWN AS WHAT?

1,211. True or false? High clouds indicate that rain is on the way.

TOUGH TRIVIA CHALLENGE

1,212. What is the world's lightest rock?
a. Sandstone
b. Pumice
c. Granite
d. Coal

1,213. The Earth's mantle is made up of what?
a. Rock
b. Dead plant matter
c. Liquid metal
d. Solid metal

1,214. What is a geyser?
a. Water heated by a volcano that flows like a river
b. Underground water heated by magma that erupts in steam
c. A type of miniature volcano that forms underground
d. Underground water cooled and compressed until forced upward

1,215. What causes a wind to blow?

a. The ocean currents

b. The rotation of the Earth

c. Too many air masses in one place

d. Differences in air pressure

1,216. Stratus clouds usually indicate what kind of weather?

a. Sunny weather

b. Any kind of weather

c. Rainy weather

d. No weather

1,217. TRUE OR FALSE? ALL ROCKS ARE MADE UP OF MINERALS.

MATCH THE FOLLOWING INSTRUMENTS WITH THE TYPE OF WEATHER THEY MEASURE:

1,218. Wind vane
1,219. Barometer
1,220. Pyranometer
1,221. Hygrometer
1,222. Rain gauge
1,223. Thermometer
1,224. Transmissometer
1,225. Wind sock
1,226. Anemometer
1,227. Ceilometer

a. Measures wind speed and direction
b. Measures solar radiation
c. Measures air and sea surface temperature
d. Measures cloud ceiling
e. Shows from where the wind is blowing
f. Measures precipitation over a specific time
g. Measures wind speed
h. Measures atmospheric pressure
i. Measures humidity
j. Measures visibility

1,227. True or false? **The Supercell is the least dangerous kind of thunderstorm.**

1,228. A rock worn down by the air and wind is said to have experienced which of these?
- a. Erosion
- b. Breakage
- c. Weathering
- d. Exhumation

1,229. The mineral pyrite is also known as what?
- a. Fake gold
- b. True gold
- c. Fool's gold
- d. Pretend gold

1,230. Which U.S. state was formed by magma pushing up to the Earth's crust?
- a. California
- b. Nebraska
- c. Hawaii
- d. Alaska

MATCH THE WORLD'S OCEANS TO THEIR SIZES, FROM LARGEST (FIRST) TO SMALLEST (FIFTH):

1,231. Pacific   a. Fifth
1,232. Arctic   b. Fourth
1,233. Indian   c. Third
1,234. Atlantic   d. First
1,235. Southern   e. Second

1,236. What is a rill?

a. Another name for a hill.
b. A small channel cut by a stream.
c. A deep channel cut by water.
d. The edge of a mountain.

MATCH THESE MOUNTAIN FEATURES WITH THEIR DESCRIPTIONS:

1,237. Face
1,238. Leeward
1,239. Horn
1,240. Pass
1,241. Ridge
1,242. Peak
1,243. Crag
1,244. Slope
1,245. Cirque
1,246. Moraine

a. The highest point of any mountain
b. Rocks and dirt left behind by glaciers
c. A bowl formed by a glacier, most often at the foot of a mountain
d. A sharp peak formed by glaciers
e. The side of a mountain protected from wind and rain
f. Rock that sticks out from a cliff or face
g. A path or a valley between mountains
h. The steep side of a mountain
i. The narrow top of a mountain or mountains
j. The side of a mountain

1,247. What are the three types of rocks?

1,248. What is the process in which water changes to a gas called?

a. Condensation
b. Evaporation
c. Condescension
d. Infiltration

1,249. Where does sand on a beach come from?

a. Sediment from flooding
b. Volcanic eruptions
c. Ocean waves grinding down rocks over time
d. Dead plant and animal matter

1,250. TRUE OR FALSE? NOCTILUCENT CLOUDS ARE ONLY VISIBLE DURING THE DAY.

MATCH THESE CONTINENTS TO THEIR SIZE, FROM LARGEST (FIRST) TO SMALLEST (FIFTH):

1,251. Africa   a. Second
1,252. Australia   b. Third
1,253. Asia   c. Fourth
1,254. South America   d. Fifth
1,255. Europe   e. First

1,256. Material that is transported and deposited in loose layers is called what?
a. Grains   b. Leftovers   c. Sediment   d. The rock table

1,257. What is the hardest mineral?

1,258. What creates the Earth's magnetic field?
a. Large, natural magnets floating in the core
b. Liquid iron moving in the outer core
c. A mixture of iron and aluminum is the mantle
d. Solid iron situated in the inner core

1,259. True or false? The Atlantic Ocean is very slowly growing bigger.

1,260. EACH MINERAL POSSESSES WHAT THREE PROPERTIES?

1,261. Rain is most often caused by which kind of pressure system?

1,262. True or false? Earth's mantle is outside of its crust.

1,263. Sedimentary rocks usually come from what?

a. Plant material
b. Erosion
c. Earthquakes
d. Lava deposits

1,264. Which mineral tastes salty?

a. Halite
b. Calcite
c. Kyanite
d. Biotite

1,265. Which of these is a type of precipitation?

a. Rain b. Hail
c. Sleet d. All of the above

1,266. Purple quartz is better known as what?

a. Black diamond
b. Amethyst
c. Rose quartz
d. Ruby

1.267. TRUE OR FALSE?
BLIZZARDS ONLY HAPPEN DURING SNOWSTORMS.

1,268. Any type of water that falls from the air is called what?

a. Condensation
b. The dew point
c. Precipitation
d. Transposition

1,269. How is igneous rock formed?

a. Wind erosion
b. Cooling lava or magma
c. Water erosion
d. Compression by other rock

1,270. What is the name of atmospheric layer where most weather occurs?

a. Ionosphere
b. Stratosphere
c. Troposphere
d. Mesosphere

Answers: 1,251. a; 1,252. d; 1,253. e; 1,254. b; 1,255. c; 1,256. c; 1,257. Diamond; 1,258. b; 1,259. True; 1,260. Luster, cleavage, and hardness; 1,261. Low pressure system; 1,262. False, the mantle is under the crust; 1,263. b; 1,264. a.; 1,265. d.; 1,266. b; 1,267. True; 1,268. c; 1,269. b; 1,270. c

Geography & Earth Science • 141

1,271. What is the world's softest mineral?

    a. Pumice

    b. Quartz

    c. Talc

    d. Diamond

1,272. Bedrock is labeled with which letter?

    a. A   b. O

    c. B   d. D

1,273. TRUE OR FALSE? THE MINERAL FLUORIDE IS USED IN TOOTHPASTE.

MATCH THE FOLLOWING METEOROLOGICAL WORDS TO THEIR DESCRIPTIONS:

1,274. Fog
1,275. Monsoon
1,276. Typhoon
1,277. Humidity
1,278. Mistral

a. A seasonal abrupt wind change, with corresponding changes in precipitation. Common in Southeast Asia.
b. The amount of water vapor present in the air.
c. A type of cyclone in the northwestern Pacific Ocean.
d. Small water droplets or ice crystals in the air at or near the ground.
e. Strong wind that blows through Southern France.

1,279. The study of weather and Earth's atmosphere is called what?

1,280. How is a caldera formed?

    a. A tidal wave

    b. An earthquake

    c. A period of erosion

    d. A collapsing volcano

1,281. The swift current on the West side of the Northern Atlantic Ocean is called what?

    a. The Nor'Easter

    b. The Western Wind

    c. The Gulf Breeze

    d. The Gulf Stream

1,282. What is the Ring of Fire?
   a. The perimeter of the Pacific Ocean, noted for volcanic activity
   b. A point where magma pours out to the Earth's surface
   c. The rim around a volcano
   d. The caldera formed by a collapsing volcano

1,283. True or false? Most minerals of the Earth's crust are made up of the same 8 elements in different amounts.

1,284. WHAT ARE TUBES OF HIGH-SPEED AIR CALLED?

1,285. About how old is the earth?
   a. 450 million years   b. 4.5 billion years
   c. 45 billion years   d. 45 million years

1,286. MOST SNOWFLAKES HAVE HOW MANY SIDES?

MATCH EACH LAYER OF THE EARTH WITH ITS DESCRIPTION:

1,287. Inner core
1,288. Crust
1,289. Tectonic plates
1,290. Mantle
1,291. Outer core

a. The solid and very hot layer
b. A thick layer, made up mostly of rocks
c. The liquid layer that produces earth's magnetic field
d. The lithosphere, moves very slowly, can cause earthquakes
e. The outer layer of the earth we live on

Answers: 1,271. c; 1,272. d; 1,273. True; 1,274. d; 1,275. a; 1,276. c; 1,277. b; 1,278. e; 1,279. Meteorology; 1,280. d; 1,281. d; 1,282. a; 1,283. True; 1,284. Jet streams; 1,285. b; 1,286. Six; 1,287. a; 1,288. e; 1,289. d; 1,290. b; 1,291. c.

Geography & Earth Science • 143

1,292. Punxsutawney Phil is associated with which holiday about the length of winter?

1,293. Which of these is caused by an underwater earthquake or landslide?
a. Water spout   b. Cyclone
c. Maelstrom   d. Tsunami

1,294. Earth's continents were once one big continent. What is it called?
a. Australasia
b. Atalan
c. Middle Earth
d. Pangaea

1,295. What is a Nor'easter?
a. A storm that starts in the West and moves East
b. A storm along the East Coast of North America
c. A storm that starts in the North and moves South
d. A storm that happens in the spring

1,296. True or false? Cinnabar is so-called because it smells like cinnamon.

MATCH EACH MINERAL PROPERTY WITH ITS DESCRIPTION:

1,297. Luster
1,298. Specific gravity
1,299. Hardness
1,300. Cleavage
1,301. Streak

a. The mineral's color in powdered form
b. How easy it is to scratch the minerals' surface
c. How a mineral breaks
d. How well a mineral reflects light
e. How dense the mineral is

1,302. WHAT IS "TORNADO ALLEY"?

1,303. True or false? **The Fujita scale measures amounts of rainfall.**

1,304. The Earth gets which of these, the deeper in you go?
   a. Gets cooler
   b. Varies in temperature
   c. Gets hotter
   d. Doesn't change much from surface temperatures

1,305. TRUE OR FALSE? THUNDER IS THE SOUND OF LIGHTNING.

1.306. IN THE SOUTHERN HEMISPHERE, WHAT HAPPENS AROUND DECEMBER 21?

1,307. True or false? **A cold front is caused by cold air sliding under warm air.**

1,308. About how many different kinds of minerals exist on earth?
   a. 300–500
   b. 1,000–2,000
   c. 3,000–5,000
   d. 6,000–8,000

1,309. Magma leaking on to the earth's surface is known as what?
   a. Intrusion
   b. Exhumation
   c. Inclusion
   d. Extrusion

1,310. What is the most common gas in earth's atmosphere?
   a. Oxygen
   b. Hydrogen
   c. Nitrogen
   d. Carbon Dioxide

Answers: 1,292. Groundhog Day; 1,293. d; 1,294. b; 1,295. b; 1,296. False, it gains its name from its reddish color; 1,297. d; 1,298. c; 1,299. b; 1,300. c; 1,301. a; 1,302. An area of the American midwest (including Texas, Oklahoma, and Kansas) that experience large amounts of tornadoes every year; 1,303. False, it measures the strength of tornadoes; 1,304. c; 1,305. True; 1,306. The first day of summer; 1,307. True; 1,308. c; 1,309. d; 1,310. c;

1,311. True or false? **All of the world's oceans are saltwater.**

1,312. What is a good definition of a rock?

1,313. WHAT IS A ZEPHYR?

1,314. What causes the tides?
   a. The Moon's gravity
   b. The Earth's rotation
   c. The Earth's gravity
   d. The Sun's gravity

1,315. If we say a wind is a "North wind," what does that mean?
   a. It blows from the South to the North
   b. It stays in the North
   c. It blows from the North to the South
   d. It blow from any direction to the North

1,316. What tool measures air pressure?
   a. Hydrometer
   b. Altimeter
   c. Barometer
   d. Thermometer

1,317. True or false? It's possible to stand inside a rainbow.

1,318. What is the name of a tornado that forms over water?

1,319. What is a Derecho?
   a. A type of hurricane
   b. A powerful winter storm in New England
   c. A series of strong storms that follow one after another
   d. A type of tornado

1,320. What kind of front brings winds and heavy rain?
   a. Differential front
   b. Cold front
   c. Backward front
   d. Warm front

1.321. TRUE OR FALSE? MOST OF THE EARTH'S FRESH WATER IS UNDERGROUND.

1,322. WHAT DOES A PLUVIOGRAPH MEASURE?

1,323. True or false? At a temperature of -40, Centigrade is equal to Fahrenheit.

1,324. Which type of weather front moves the fastest?

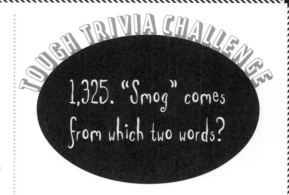

TOUGH TRIVIA CHALLENGE

1,325. "Smog" comes from which two words?

1,326. What is another name for the aurora borealis?

1,327. True or false? **The Earth bulges a bit at the equator.**

1.328. "RED SKY AT NIGHT, SAILOR'S (OR SHEPHERD'S) DELIGHT" MEANS WHAT?

1,329. A microscale describes what weather phenomenon?
   a. Hurricane   b. Tornado
   c. Cyclone   d. Thunderstorm

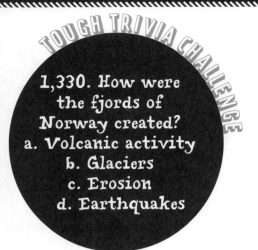

1,330. How were the fjords of Norway created?
a. Volcanic activity
b. Glaciers
c. Erosion
d. Earthquakes

1,331. What does coal come from?
a. Dead plant matter
b. Pulverized rock
c. Dead animal matter
d. Crushed diamonds

1,332. What is the natural laying down of rock-forming material called?
a. Formation
b. Settling
c. Deposition
d. Disruption

1,333. Where can we find graphite every day?
a. In tires on cars
b. In sodas
c. In pencil lead
d. In shampoo

1,334. Who is the father of modern geology?
a. Nicholas Steno
b. Charles Lyell
c. James Hutton
d. George Gibbs

1,335. A hurricane dies down when what happens?
a. It comes into contact with the Gulf Stream
b. It moves out to sea
c. It moves over land or cold water
d. Winter weather arrives

1,336. Hurricanes come from where?
   a. Over the mountains and then move to sea
   b. Over cold water
   c. Over the Southern Ocean and move north
   d. Over warm water

1,337. Cirrus clouds are made out of what?
   a. Smoke
   b. Water vapor
   c. Mist
   d. Ice crystals

1,338. What does Earth's ozone layer do?
   a. Protects us from infrared radiation
   b. Allows clouds to form
   c. Protects us from ultraviolet radiation
   d. Keeps the Earth at a stable temperature

1,339. TRUE OR FALSE? EARTH'S INNER CORE IS SOLID.

1,340. What percentage of the diamonds mined in the world can be made into gems?

a. 20–30%
b. 10–15%
c. 35%
d. 50%

1,341. What is the surface water during and after it rains called?

a. Infiltration
b. Flooding
c. Runoff
d. Hydration

TOUGH TRIVIA CHALLENGE

1,342. Molten rock that pours out of a volcano is called what?

a. Pourage
b. Lava
c. Element slush
d. Magma

1,343. When plants give water back to the atmosphere, what is it called?

a. Inspiration
b. Transpiration
c. Perspiration
d. Evaporation

1,344. What is the movement of water through the soil and into the ground called?

a. Flooding
b. Inltration
c. Flow
d. Seepage

1,345. What are the flat surfaces of crystals called?

a. Cuts   b. Faces
c. Facets   d. Sides

1,346. Who proposed these three important geological principles: the principles of superposition, original horizontality, and lateral continuity?

a. Isaac Newton

b. James Hutton

c. Nicholas Steno

d. René Descartes

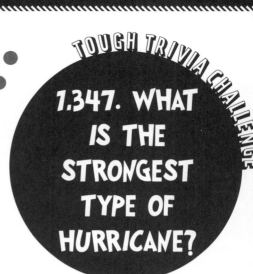

TOUGH TRIVIA CHALLENGE

1,347. WHAT IS THE STRONGEST TYPE OF HURRICANE?

1,348. How was Giant's Causeway in Northern Ireland formed?
a. Water   b. Erosion
c. Volcanic eruption   d. Earthquake

1,349. Which of these is a sedimentary rock?

a. Granite

b. Soapstone

c. Sandstone

d. Marble

1,350. When sand is heated, it becomes what?

a. Granite

b. Coal

c. Diamonds

d. Glass

Answers: 1,340. a; 1,341. c; 1,342. b; 1,343. b; 1,344. b; 1,345. b; 1,346. c; 1,347. Category 5; 1,348. c; 1,349. c; 1,350. d

Geography & Earth Science • 151

CHAPTER 4

Mythology

1,351. Aphrodite is married to which god?
- a. Zeus
- b. Hephaestus
- c. Apollo
- d. Hades

1,352. What did Dionysus grant to King Midas?
- a. Rulership over all of ancient Greece
- b. The power to turn things to gold by toughing them
- c. Immortality
- d. The power to kill things by touching them

1,353. Who is Charon?
- a. The last of the Titans
- b. The servant of Ares
- c. The ferryman to the Underworld
- d. The guard at the gates of Hades

1,354. THE RULERS OF THE WORLD BEFORE THE GREEK GODS WERE KNOWN AS WHAT?
- A. TITANS
- B. IMMORTALS
- C. ETERNALS
- D. GIANTS

1,355. Which tree was considered sacred in ancient Athens?
- a. Maple
- b. Olive
- c. Pine
- d. Oak

1,356. Pan plays what instrument?
- a. Cymbals
- b. Drum
- c. Pipes
- d. Lyre

1,357. Aphrodite's son is named what?

a. Theseus   b. Eros

c. Cronus   d. Perseus

1,358. TRUE OR FALSE?
THOR *IS* THE SON OF ODIN.

MATCH THE FOLLOWING GREEK GODS AND GODDESSES TO THEIR DOMAINS:

1,359. Aphrodite   a. Reason and wisdom
1,360. Dionysus   b. Music, the sun
1,361. Poseidon   c. Love
1,362. Artemis   d. The hunt and wilderness
1,363. Hades   e. Harvest, agriculture
1,364. Athena   f. Wine
1,365. Ares   g. War
1,366. Demeter   h. Travel, communication
1,367. Hermes   i. The sea
1,368. Apollo   j. The Underworld

1,369. On what island were the Minotaur and the labyrinth?

- - - - - - - -

1,370. In Chinese mythology, who is the Jade Emperor?

a. The ruler of China
b. The ruler of the sea
c. The ruler of the universe
d. The ruler of the mountains

1,371. What were Mesopotamian temples called?

a. Mausoleums   b. Pyramids
c. Ziggurats   d. Shrines

- - - - - - - -

1,372. The thunderbird is a legendary creature from which tradition?

a. Middle Eastern   b. Indian
c. Native American   d. African

1,373. True or false? Cats were sacred animals to ancient Egyptians.

MATCH THE FOLLOWING NORSE GODS AND GODDESSES TO THEIR DOMAINS:

1,374. Njord	a. War
1,375. Thor	b. Eloquence
1,376. Heimdall	c. Thunder
1,377. Hel	d. The sea
1,378. Odin	e. Poetry and death
1,379. Tyr	f. Fertility
1,380. Loki	g. Guardian of the Bifrost Bridge
1,381. Balder	h. Fire and mischief
1,382. Freya	i. The Underworld
1,383. Bragi	j. Beauty

1,384. THE NAME OF THE GREEK GOD PAN GIVES US WHICH WORD MEANING "SUDDEN FEAR"?

1,385. Anansi is a trickster spider figure in which region of the world?
a. North America   b. West Africa   c. South Australia   d. Central Asia

Answers: 1,357. b; 1,358. True; 1,359. c; 1,360. f; 1,361. i; 1,362. d; 1,363. j; 1,364. a; 1,365. g; 1,366. e; 1,367. h; 1,368. b; 1,369. Crete; 1,370. c; 1,371. c; 1,372. c; 1,373. True; 1,374. d; 1,375. c; 1,376. g; 1,377. i; 1,378. e; 1,379. a; 1,380. h; 1,381. j; 1,382. f; 1,383. b; 1,384. Panic; 1,385. b.

Mythology • 755

1,386. In Chinese myth, Kwan Yin is goddess of what?
- a. Mercy and compassion
- b. Commerce
- c. Love
- d. Feasting and celebration

◆ ◆ ◆ ◆ ◆ ◆ ◆ ◆ ◆ ◆ ◆ ◆ ◆

1,387. Who is the best friend of Gilgamesh?
- **a. Enlil**
- **b. Enkidu**
- **c. Shamash**
- **d. Anu**

◆ ◆ ◆ ◆ ◆ ◆ ◆ ◆ ◆ ◆ ◆ ◆ ◆

1,388. In Babylonian myth, who is Tiamat?
- a. A mother goddess
- b. A dragon of the first sea
- c. The queen of the gods
- d. The goddess of the earth

◆ ◆ ◆ ◆ ◆ ◆ ◆ ◆ ◆ ◆ ◆ ◆ ◆

1,389. TRUE OR FALSE? ECHO IS A WOOD NYMPH WHO TALKED TOO MUCH.

◆ ◆ ◆ ◆ ◆ ◆ ◆ ◆ ◆ ◆ ◆ ◆ ◆

1,390. What was the Greek Titan Atlas cursed to do?

1,391. True or false? Set and Osiris were allies.

◆ ◆ ◆ ◆ ◆ ◆ ◆ ◆ ◆ ◆ ◆ ◆ ◆

1,392. In Irish myth, who is the Dagda?
- a. A famed Irish chief
- b. Leader of the Irish gods
- c. Leader of the Fomorians
- d. A famous Irish hero, known for his bravery

1,393. In some Egyptian myths, what was significant about the god Ptah?
- **a. He was the father of all the gods**
- **b. He ruled over all of Egypt after becoming the first pharaoh**
- **c. He fought with Osiris over who would wed Isis**
- **d. He created the world by saying words and bringing it to life**

1,393. What is unusual about Odin?

a. He has one leg
b. He is blind in one eye
c. He has one arm
d. He cannot grow a beard

1,395. Quetzalcoatl, the god of wind and wisdom, was worshipped by which group?

a. The Sumerians
b. The Chinese
c. The Egyptians
d. The Aztecs

1,396. True or false? The pharaoh Akhenaten banned all other Egyptian gods and decreed that only the sun god, Aten, was to be worshipped.

1,397. What is the name of Arthur's primary castle?

a. Glastonbury
b. Cadbury
c. Camelot
d. Avalon

1,398. Who is Arthur's father?

a. Gawain
b. Merlin
c. Mordred
d. Uther Pendragon

1,399. In Irish myth, a female spirit who wails for a coming death is called what?

a. Selkie   b. Kobold
c. Pixie   d. Banshee

1,400. In Ireland, what are the sidhe?

a. A name for the water fairies
b. Earth mounds where fairies lived
c. Mountains of the gods
d. Forests that are home to magical creatures

1,401. What were the preserved bodies of the dead called in ancient Egypt?

a. Corpses   b. Mummies
c. Life dolls   d. Effigies

Answers: 1,386. a; 1,387. b; 1,388. b; 1,389.True; 1,390. He holds up the heavens on his shoulders forever; 1,391. False. Set murders Osiris and tries to usurp his throne; 1,392. b; 1,393. d; 1,395. d; 1,396.True; 1,397. c; 1,398. d; 1,399. d; 1,400. b; 1,401. b.

1,402. The pharaoh was believed to be a human manifestation of which god?

a. Bes

b. Horus

c. Ra

d. Osiris

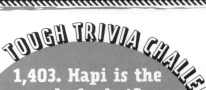

TOUGH TRIVIA CHALLENGE

1,403. Hapi is the god of what?
a. The rare rains
b. The sitting sun
c. The arrival of spring
d. The annual flooding of the Nile

MATCH THE FOLLOWING EGYPTIAN GODS AND GODDESSES TO THEIR DOMAINS:

1,404. Khonshu   a. The Sun

1,405. Bastet   b. Knowledge and writing

1,406. Anubis   c. Cats, protection

1,407. Ra   d. Chaos

1,408. Isis   e. War

1,409. Horus   f. The Moon

1,410. Set   g. Funerals

1,411. Osiris   h. The sky

1,412. Thoth   i. The Underworld, the dead

1,413. Sekhmet   j. Magic, protection

1,414. HOW LONG DID ODIN HANG FROM A TREE TO GAIN THE RUNES?

1,415. In Sumerian myth, Inanna was goddess of what?

    a. Spring and summer
    b. Food and drink
    c. Love and war
    d. Music and dance

▲ ▲ ▲ ▲ ▲ ▲ ▲ ▲ ▲ ▲ ▲ ▲ ▲ ▲

1,416. What was probably the most important musical instrument of Irish myth?

a. **The drum**   b. **The flute**
c. **The whistle** d. **The harp**

▲ ▲ ▲ ▲ ▲ ▲ ▲ ▲ ▲ ▲ ▲ ▲ ▲ ▲

1,417. Horus fought who to avenge his father, Osiris?

    a. Isis   b. Nut
    c. Set   d. Sekhmet

▲ ▲ ▲ ▲ ▲ ▲ ▲ ▲ ▲ ▲ ▲ ▲ ▲ ▲

1,418. What will happen after Ragnarok?

    a. The old gods will be restored
    b. A new world and new gods will arise
    c. The universe will be dark forever
    d. The giants will rule the world

1,419. In Norse myth, who fought against the Vanir?

    a. The Vikings
    b. The Aesir
    c. The Giants
    d. The Elves

▲ ▲ ▲ ▲ ▲ ▲ ▲ ▲ ▲ ▲ ▲ ▲ ▲ ▲

1,420. Which of Arthur's knights was known as the "Perfect Knight"?

1,421. The Greek goddess of the earth was named what?

    a. Geb
    b. Terpsichore
    c. Demeter
    d. Gaea

1,422. In ancient Egypt, Ma'at was a goddess, but also which of these?

    a. A pharaoh of Egypt in her own right
    b. The concept of truth, order, and justice
    c. A human woman, wife of an important pharaoh
    d. The ideal of what a goddess should be

1,423. Amun was, at first, the most important of the Egyptian gods, but was later combined with which other god?

a. Aten   b. Ra
c. Nut   d. Geb

1,424. What is a scarab?

a. A beetle
b. A scorpion
c. A fly
d. A wasp

1,425. Who gives Arthur his sword?

a. Merlin
b. The Lady of the Lake
c. Morgan le Fay
d. Guinevere

1.426. THE LAND OF THE NORSE GODS WAS KNOWN AS WHAT?

1,427. What ancient object do Arthur's knights search for?

a. The Necklace of Dreams
b. The Gordian Knot
c. The Spear of Destiny
d. The Holy Grail

1,428. What is the name of King Arthur's sword?

a. Sting
b. Glamdring
c. Excalibur
d. Mjolnir

1,429. What was the Morrígan the goddess of in ancient Ireland?

a. The harvest
b. The dead
c. Battle
d. Love

1,430. TRUE OR FALSE? MORDRED KILLS KING ARTHUR

1,431. In Egyptian myth, the heart of a dead person was weighed in the afterlife against what item to determine if the soul was worthy?

1,432. What is special about Odin's horse, Sleipnir?

a. He has wings
b. He has a human head
c. He is made of fire
d. He has eight legs

1,433. Who are the Norns?
a. Warriors of Midgard
b. Elves who fight for the gods
c. Mysterious female beings who control destiny
d. Handmaidens of Odin who bring the dead to Valhalla

1,434. In the legend of King Arthur, who must face the Green Knight?

1,435. True or false? Odin created the first two humans from rocks.

1,436. What was unusual in depictions of the Egyptian dwarf god, Bes?

a. He always had at least two other gods on either side of him
b. He was normally shown facing forward, unlike the other gods, who faced sideways
c. His face was never shown out of respect
d. He was very tall

1,437. TRUE OR FALSE? THE ANIMAL THAT THE EGYPTIAN GOD SET REPRESENTS IS UNKNOWN.

Answers: 1,423. b; 1,424. a; 1,425. b; 1,426. Asgard; 1,427. d; 1,428. c; 1,429. c; 1,430. True; 1,431. A feather; 1,432. d; 1,433. c; 1,434. Gawain; 1,435. False; Odin created the first two humans from trees; 1,436. b; 1,437. True

Mythology • 161

1,438. What day of the week is named for the Norse god of thunder?

....

1,439. In Norse myth, what is Midgard?
    a. "Middle Kingdom," a land of the gods
    b. "Middle Mountains," home of the dwarves
    c. "Middle Earth," the world of humanity
    d. "Middle Forest," land of the elves

1,440. In Greek myth, who was the handsome man who fell in love with his own reflection?
    a. Ganymede
    b. Paris
    c. Perseus
    d. Narcissus

1,441. What part of the body was the one weakness of the hero Achilles?
a. His big toe   b. His heel
c. His arm   d. His hand

1,442. True or false? Most ancient Egyptians only worshipped one god at a time.

1,443. What direction do the souls of the ancient Egyptian dead travel to be judged?

1,444. In Norse myth, what is the relationship of the giants to the gods?
    a. They are friends
    b. They are enemies
    c. The gods are the giants' teachers
    d. The giants are the gods' teachers

....

1,445. A Viking warrior who falls in battle may join Odin in the afterlife where?
    a. Jotunheim   b. Hel
    c. Valhalla   d. Niflheim

1,446. The end of all things in Norse myth is known as what?

    a. The Bifrost   b. Loki's Bane

    c. Helheim   d. Ragnarok

1,447. In Norse myth, what is Alfheim?

a. The home of the new gods

b. The home of the Dark Elves

c. The home of the old gods

d. The home of the Light Elves

1,448. Thor carries which of these as a weapon?

a. Knife   b. Hammer   c. Sword   d. Spear

1,449. What was the ancient Egyptian symbol of life called?

    a. Cross   b. Pentagram

    c. Crescent   d. Ankh

1,450. True or false? *Balor was a hero in Irish legend.*

Answers: 1,438. Thursday; 1,439. c; 1,440. d; 1,441. b; 1,442. False, they worshiped multiple gods; 1,443. West; 1,444. b; 1,445. c; 1,446. d; 1,447. d; 1,448. b; 1,449. d; 1,450. False, he was a tyrant leader.

Mythology • **163**

CHAPTER 5

Sports & Games

OLYMPIC SPORTS

1,451. The top eight athletes in each Olympic event receive what from the IOC?
- a. A medal
- b. A diploma
- c. Flowers
- d. Money

1,452. The Summer and Winter Games are both held how often?
- a. Every five years
- b. Every two years
- c. Every four years
- d. Every three years

1,453. How many medals are awarded for each Olympic event?
- a. Two
- b. Three
- c. Four
- d. One

1,454. TRUE OR FALSE? NADIA COMĂNECI NEVER COMPETED IN ANOTHER OLYMPICS AFTER HER PERFECT SCORE IN MONTREAL IN 1976.

1,455. What was the first year in which all the participating nations sent female athletes?
- a. 1996
- b. 1988
- c. 2012
- d. 2000

1,456. The first Paralympic Games of 1948 were held where?
- a. London
- b. Paris
- c. New York
- d. Athens

Answers: 1,451. b; 1,452. c; 1,453. b; 1,454. False, she also competed in the 1980 and 1984 Summer Olympics; 1,455. c; 1,456. a.

1,457. The pentathlon includes which of the following sports?

a. Shooting   b. Horseback riding   c. Fencing   d. All of the above

---

1,458. True or false? As of 2022, no country in the Southern Hemisphere has hosted a Winter Olympics.

MATCH THE FOLLOWING OLYMPIC ATHLETES WITH THEIR SPORTS:

1,459. Chris Hoy, Great Britain	a. Cross-country skiing
1,460. Nadia Comăneci, Romania	b. Men's figure skating
1,461. Jesse Owens, United States	c. Swimming
1,462. Lindsey Vonn, United States	d. Cycling
1,463. Michael Phelps, United States	e. Boxing
1,464. Kerri Walsh Jennings, United States	f. Beach volleyball
1,465. Greg Louganis, United States	g. Track and field
1,466. Venus Williams, United States	h. Women's figure skating
1,467. Caitlyn Jenner, United States	i. Speedskating
1,468. Birgit Fischer, Germany	j. Diving
1,469. Aleksandr Karelin, Russia	k. Alpine ski racer
1,470. Marit Bjørgen, Norway	l. Women's gymnastics
1,471. Joe Frazier, United States	m. Tennis
1,472. Kristi Yamaguchi, United States	n. Snowboarding
1,473. Shaun White, United States	o. Men's gymnastics
1,474. Elisabeta Lipă, Romania	p. Rowing
1,475. Evgeni Plushenko, Russia	l. Shooting
1,476. Kim Rhode, United States	q. Kayaking
1,477. Alexei Nemov, Russia	r. Decathlon
1,478. Claudia Pechstein, Germany	s. Greco-roman wrestling

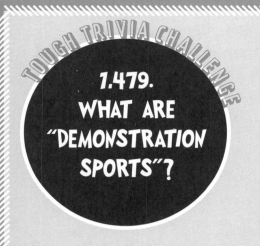

1,479. WHAT ARE "DEMONSTRATION SPORTS"?

1,480. Hans-Gunnar Liljenwall became the first Olympic athlete to be disqualified for using a drug. What did he consume?

    a. Alcohol   b. Cocaine
    c. Heroin   d. Tobacco

1,481. Women's fencing became an Olympic sport in what year?

    a. 1912 b. 1924
    c. 1956 d. 1972

1,482. Who boycotted the 1980 Moscow Summer Olympics?

    a. Great Britain   b. India
    c. United States   d. China

1,483. How many hours was the longest wrestling match in modern Olympic history?

    a. 2 hours   b. 4 hours   c. 7 hours   d. 11 hours

1,484. Which winter sport takes place over two days, and features both ski jumping and cross country skiing?

    a. Biathlon   b. Decathlon
    c. Nordic Combined   d. Slalom

Answers: 1,457. d; 1,458.True; 1,459. d; 1,460. l; 1,461. g; 1,462. k; 1,463. c; 1,464. f; 1,465. j; 1,466. m; 1,467. r; 1,468. q; 1,469. s; 1,470. a; 1,471. e; 1,472. h; 1,473. n; 1,474. p; 1,475. b; 1,476. i; 1,477. o; 1,478. i; 1,479. Non-medal events that showcase the host nations' unique sporting life; 1,480. a; 1,481. b; 1,482. c; 1,483. d; 1,484. c.

1,485. What was the year of the first ancient Olympics?
- a. 110 BCE
- b. 15 CE
- c. 776 BCE
- d. 345 BCE

◆ ◆ ◆ ◆ ◆ ◆ ◆ ◆ ◆ ◆ ◆

1,486. True or false? The nation hosting the Games that year marches first in the opening ceremony.

◆ ◆ ◆ ◆ ◆ ◆ ◆ ◆ ◆ ◆ ◆

1,487. What does the Olympic motto "Citius, Altius, Fortius" mean in English?

◆ ◆ ◆ ◆ ◆ ◆ ◆ ◆ ◆ ◆ ◆

1,488. What are the official languages of the Olympic games?
- a. Greek and English, plus the language of the host country
- b. English and French, plus the language of the host country
- c. Greek and French, plus the language of the host country
- d. English and Greek, plus the language of the host country

1,489. Why were three Summer Olympics cancelled in the past?
- a. Boycotts by too many nations
- b. Wars
- c. Lack of money
- d. Lack of attendance

◆ ◆ ◆ ◆ ◆ ◆ ◆ ◆ ◆ ◆ ◆

1,490. True or false? Ice hockey first appeared at the 1920 Summer Olympics.

◆ ◆ ◆ ◆ ◆ ◆ ◆ ◆ ◆ ◆ ◆

1,491. What is athlete Christa Luding-Rothenburger's Olympic claim to fame?

1,492. Which of these colors is in the Olympic rings?
- a. Purple
- b. Orange
- c. Blue
- d. Magenta

1,493. At the 1900 Paris Olympics...
a. The athletes wore no clothing when competing
b. There was chariot racing
c. There were more athletes than spectators
d. There were no women athletes

◆◆◆◆◆◆◆◆◆◆◆◆◆◆◆◆◆

1,494. The five Olympic rings represent what?
a. The five founders of the modern Olympics
b. Five continents
c. Five centuries of competition
d. The five countries that initiated the modern Olympics

1,495. Which of the following is a Paralympic sport primarily for the visually impaired?
a. Boccia   b. Curling
c. Goalball   d. Dressage

◆◆◆◆◆◆◆◆◆◆◆◆◆◆◆◆◆

1,496. Athletes at the ancient Olympics wore what?
a. Robes   b. Togas
c. Loin cloths   d. Nothing

◆◆◆◆◆◆◆◆◆◆◆◆◆◆◆◆◆◆◆◆◆◆◆◆◆◆◆

MATCH THE FOLLOWING OLYMPIC SPORTS TO THEIR DESCRIPTIONS:

1,497. Biathlon

1,498. Parallel Giant Slalom

1,499. Women's Heptathlon

1,500. Curling

1,501. Triathlon

1,502. Nordic Combined

1,503. Moguls

1,504. Pentathlon

1,505. Men's Heptathlon

1,506. Giant slalom

a. Ski jumping and cross-country skiing
b. Downhill snowboarding
c. Skiing and shooting
d. Skiing over low snow mounds
e. Skiing downhill between sets of poles
f. Swimming, running, and cycling
g. 100-meter hurdles, high jump, shot put, 200 meters, long jump, javelin, and 800 meters
h. 60 meters, long jump, shot put, high jump, 60-meter hurdles, and 1000 meters
i. Sliding stones on ice
j. Fencing, swimming, horse riding, shooting, and running

1,507. At the first Olympics, Koroibos won the stadion (foot race). What was his occupation?

    a. Farmer   b. Politician   c. Cook   d. Soldier

1,508. As of 2016, which nation has won the most gold medals in men's archery?

    a. United States   b. Great Britain
    c. Belgium   d. Germany

1,509. The Paralympic Games take place when?
    a. Before the Summer Olympics
    b. After the Summer Olympics
    c. During the Summer Olympics
    d. In the same year as the Summer Olympics

1,510. How many gold medals did Carl Lewis win for the long jump?

    a. Three   b. Four   c. Two   d. Five

1,511. Which of these is not a Summer Olympics sport?

    a. Water polo   b. Badminton
    c. Motorcycle racing   d. Taekwondo

1,512. Margaret Abbott was the first American woman to win an Olympic gold medal, in 1900, for which sport?

a. Rowing b. Golf

c. Tennis   d. Swimming

1,513. WHAT ARE THE COLORS OF THE OLYMPIC RINGS?

1,514. The ancient Olympic Games had a sport called Pankration; what was it?

a. Combined marathon and chariot racing
b. Combined sprinting and chariot racing
c. Combined boxing and wrestling
d. Combined swimming and wrestling

1,515. Where did the first Special Olympics International Summer Games of 1968 take place?

a. New York b. Atlanta
c. Chicago   d. Los Angeles

1,516. During the ancient Games, the pan–Hellenic truce (when no one would fight or go to war) lasted for how long?

a. 3 months
b. 3 weeks
c. 1 month
d. 1 year

1,517. TRUE OR FALSE? WATER MOTORSPORTS USED TO BE AN OLYMPIC EVENT?

1,518. What are the four indoor sports of the Winter Olympics?

1,519. What is another name for the gymnastic pommel horse?

a. The donkey b. The mule
c. The pig   d. The hippo

Answers: 1,507. c; 1,508. c; 1,509. c; 1,510. a; 1,511. c; 1,512. b; 1,513. Blue, yellow, black, green, and red; 1,514. c; 1,515. c; 1,516. a; 1,517.True; 1,518. ice hockey, figure skating, speed skating, and curling; 1,519. c

1,520. The "The Dream Team" referred to which American Olympic sports team?
a. Soccer
b. Basketball
c. Bobsleigh
d. Baseball

1,521. In which Olympic sport do men and women compete against each other as equals?
a. Archery
b. Shooting
c. Equestrian events
d. Skiing

1,522. True or false? As of 2018, Norway has won more gold medals at the Winter Games than any other country.

1,523. HOW OLD WAS THE YOUNGEST-EVER OLYMPIC MEDAL WINNER?

1,524. About how many countries compete in each Olympic Games?
a. 125   b. 200
c. 150   d. 75

1,525. True or false? Tug-of-War used to be an Olympic sport.

1,526. The modern Summer Olympics began in Athens, Greece in which year?
a. 1900   b. 1896
c. 1892   d. 1902

1,527. The modern Winter Olympics began in Chamonix, France in which year?
a. 1924   b. 1922
c. 1928   d. 1920

1,528. The original Olympic Games took place in which country?
a. Rome   b. Greece
c. Egypt   d. Sumeria

1,529. True or false?
The Olympics have been hosted in Africa.

▲▲▲▲▲▲▲▲▲▲▲

1,530. What Olympic event includes such moves as the crane, the flamingo, and the fishtail?

▲▲▲▲▲▲▲▲▲▲▲

1,531. When was the last year an athlete won the cross-country skiing event with all-wooden skis?
  a. 1956
  b. 1968
  c. 1972
  d. 1980

▲▲▲▲▲▲▲▲▲▲▲

1,532. Which Jamaican team made its famous debut at the 1988 Winter Olympics?
  a. Curling
  b. Bobsled
  c. Skiing
  d. Ice Hockey

1,533. TRUE OR FALSE?
THE 1956 WINTER GAMES IN CORTINA D'AMPEZZO, ITALY, WERE THE FIRST TO BE SHOW ON TELEVISION.

▲▲▲▲▲▲▲▲▲▲▲

1,534. The biathlon combines which two sports?
  a. Skiing and skating
  b. Skiing and rifle shooting
  c. Skating and rifle shooting
  d. Ski jumping and cross-country skiing

TOUGH TRIVIA CHALLENGE

1,535. Which continent has never hosted the Winter Olympics?
  a. Africa
  b. South America
  c. Australia
  d. All of the above

Answers: 1,520. b; 1,521. c; 1,522. True; 1,523. 7, an unnamed French boy in 1900 that helped the Dutch rowing team win; 1,524. b; 1,525. True; 1,526. b; 1,527. a; 1,528. b; 1,529. False, however Senegal will host the Summer Olympics in 2022; 1,530. Synchronized swimming; 1,531. c; 1,532. b; 1,533. True; 1,534. b; 1,535. d, however, Africa will host the 2022 Summer Olympics.

Sports & Games • **173**

MATCH THE FOLLOWING LEADERS WITH THE OLYMPICS THEY OPENED:

1,536. Queen Elizabeth II   a. Italy, 2006

1,537 William Deane   b. Montreal, 1976

1,538. Juan Carlos I   c. Beijing, 2008

1,539. Leonid Brezhnev   d. Barcelona, 1992

1,540. Akihito   e. Sydney, 2000

1,541. Carlo Azeglio Ciampi   f. Seoul, 1988

1,542. Roh Tae-woo   g. Nagano, 1998

1,543. Michel Temer   h. Moscow, 1980

1,544. Bill Clinton   i. Atlanta, 1996

1,545. Hu Jintao   j. Brazil, 2016

1,546. Which country has the most cities that have submitted bids to host the Olympics?

1,547. The Olympic "gold" medal is made mostly of what?
a. Bronze   b. Copper   c. Silver   d. Steel

1,548. Which American city hosted the Winter Olympics twice?
a. Squaw Valley
b. Salt Lake City
c. Denver
d. Lake Placid

1,549. Melbourne hosted the 1956 Summer Olympics, but the equestrian events were held in which city?
a. Stockholm   b. Sydney
c. Auckland   d. Hong Kong

1,550. The word "mogul" comes from the Austrian word "mugel," which means what?

a. Snow

b. Slope

c. Small hill or mound

d. Mountain

1,551. In 1980s' "Miracle on Ice," the U.S. Hockey team defeated which team for the gold medal?

a. Sweden

b. Norway

c. Soviet Union

d. Canada

1,552. True or false? As of 2018, the United States is the only country to have won a gold medal at every Winter Olympics.

1,553. Which woman was the only American athlete to win a gold medal at the 1968 Winter Olympics?

1,554. What was the last year that the Summer and Winter Olympics were held in the same year?

a. 1990   b. 1992

c. 1994   d. 1988

1,555. The ancient Olympics had a competition for which kind of musical instrument?

a. The lyre   b. The drum

c. The pipes   d. The trumpet

1.556. TRUE OR FALSE? WHEN PASSING THE OLYMPIC TORCH, ONLY THE FLAME IS TRANSFERRED TO A NEW CARRIER.

1,557. Which city as hosted the Summer Olympics three times?
a. Athens   b. Los Angeles
c. London   d. Paris

1,558. How many nations competed in the first modern Olympics of 1896?
a. 12   b. 14
c. 17   d. 24

1,559. True or false? Italy has competed in all 23 Winter Olympics.

1,560. Which city has submitted the most bids without ever getting to host the Olympics?

1,561. Why did Bobby Pearce slow his rowing at the 1928 Olympics?
a. His boat turned over
b. He lost an oar
c. To let a family of ducks swim by
d. He had an allergy attack

1,562. Gold medal-winning skier Alberto Tomba has what nickname?
a. El Presidente
b. Mysterio
c. La Bomba
d. La Magnifico

1,563. Who is the youngest athlete to win a gold medal at the Winter Olympics?
a. Katarina Witt
b. Kristi Yamaguchi
c. Tara Lipinski
d. Sasha Cohen

1,564. Which was the first Canadian city to host the Winter Olympics?
a. Vancouver   b. Calgary
c. Edmonton   d. Toronto

1,565. TRUE OR FALSE? FENCING WAS ADDED TO THE SUMMER OLYMPICS IN ROME IN 1960.

MATCH THE FOLLOWING OLYMPIC CITY WITH THE SEASONS AND YEARS THEY HOSTED THE GAMES:

1,566. Barcelona, Spain	a. Winter, 1968
1,567. Salt Lake City, United States	b. Winter, 1998
1,568. Sydney, Australia	c. Winter, 1964
1,569. Vancouver, Canada	d. Summer, 1988
1,570. Nagano, Japan	e. Summer, 1996
1,571. Atlanta, United States	f. Summer, 1992
1,572. Lake Placid, United States	g. Summer, 2000
1,573. Rome, Italy	h. Winter, 1984
1,574. Grenoble, France	i. Summer, 1960
1,575. London, United Kingdom	j. Summer, 2012
1,576. Turin, Italy	k. Summer, 2008
1,577. Stockholm, Sweden	l. Winter, 2002
1,578. Chamonix, France	m. Winter, 1980
1,579. Beijing, China	n. Summer, 1912
1,580. Innsbruck, Austria	o. Summer, 1980
1,581. Los Angeles, United States	p. Winter, 2006
1,582. Sarajevo, Yugoslvia	q. Winter, 1924
1,583. Moscow, Russia	r. Winter, 1972
1,584. Sapporo, Japan	s. Winter, 2010
1,585. Seoul, South Korea	t. Summer, 1984

TOUGH TRIVIA CHALLENGE

1,586. Which of the following were competitive events at the Olympics of 1912?
- a. Sculpture
- b. Painting
- c. Music
- d. All of the above

1,587. True or false? **In the 2016 Summer Games, the IOC created a team for displaced athletes.**

1,588. Why was marathon runner Fred Lorz banned for life from competing during the 1904 Summer Olympics?

1,589. What does IOC stand for?
- a. International Olympic Community
- b. Internal Olympic Chair
- c. International Olympic Committee
- d. Illustrious Olympic Champions

1,590. WHAT WAS THE SIGNIFICANCE OF OSCAR SWAHN?

1,591. Who headed committee for the opening ceremonies for the 1960 Winter Olympics?
- a. Frank Sinatra
- b. Walt Disney
- c. Rock Hudson
- d. Elvis Presley

1,592. In what year was the Olympic flag first flown?
- a. 1896
- b. 1924
- c. 1920
- d. 1900

1.593. TRUE OR FALSE? GOLF WAS AN OLYMPIC SPORT IN 1900.

1,594. When an athlete wins the gold medal music is played at the award ceremony?

1,595. The Roman Emperor Theodosius I effectively ended the original Olympic Games in what year?

    a. 100 CE
    b. 412 CE
    c. 393 CE
    d. 55 BCE

1,596. Tennis was reinstated as an *Olympic sport* in which year?

    a. 1988 b. 1972
    c. 1956 d. 1948

1,597. True or false? American football is a Winter Olympics sport.

1,598. What is the importance of the Wenlock Games?

1,599. True or false? Women were first allowed to compete in the 1900 Olympics.

1,600. What was the significance of Constantin Henriquez, who competed in the 1900 Olympics?

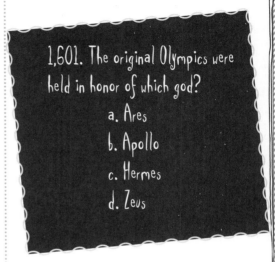

1,601. The original Olympics were held in honor of which god?

    a. Ares
    b. Apollo
    c. Hermes
    d. Zeus

1,602. True or false? Australia and New Zealand have both won medals at the Winter Olympics.

1,603. As of 2018, Bangladesh is the most populated country to have never done what at the Olympics?

Answers: 1,586. d; 1,587. True, the Refugee Olympic Team competed in the 2016 Games; 1,588. He hitched a ride in a car for most of the race, and only ran the last 4 miles; 1,589. c; 1,590. He was the oldest athlete to compete at the Olympics; 1,591. b; 1,592. c; 1,593. True; 1,594. The national anthem of their country; 1,595. c; 1,596. a; 1,597. False, it was included in the Summer Olympic Games of 1904 and 1932; 1,598. They were the forerunner of the modern Olympic Games; 1,599. True; 1,600. He was the first black athlete to do so; 1,601. d; 1,602. True; 1,603. Never to have won a medal

1,604. What was the first African city to make a bid to host the Olympics?

1,605. WHICH DUO EARNED PERFECT SCORES FOR ARTISTRY IN FIGURE SKATING AT THE 1984 WINTER OLYMPICS?

1,606. True or false? Iceland has hosted the Winter Olympics.

1,607. Eddie Eagan is the only person to have done what?

1,608. What black Olympic athlete's performance upset Hitler's desire to show Aryan supremacy in 1936?

1,609. True or false? Swimming has been an event at every modern Summer Olympics.

1,610. Baseball became an official Olympic sport in which year?
    a. 1912   b. 1928   c. 1960   d. 1992

BOARD & TABLETOP GAMES

1,611. In chess, which piece is the most powerful on the board?
a. King   b. Queen
c. Rook   d. Bishop

1,612. How many triple word score squares are there on a Scrabble board?
a. 4   b. 8
c. 12   d. 16

1,613. In Clue, how many rooms are there on the board?
a. 8
b. 9
c. 10
d. 12

MATCH THE FOLLOWING GAME PIECES WITH THEIR GAMES:

1,614. Pawn
1,615. Spy
1,616. Top hat
1,617. Tile
1,618. Follower
1,619. Lead pipe
1,620. Wedges or pie wedges
1,621. Elephant
1,622. Automobile, car
1,623. Carrier

a. Dominoes
b. Chess
c. The Game of Life
d. Carcassonne
e. Stratego
f. Battleship
g. Monopoly
h. Clue
i. Trivial Pursuit
j. Chaturanga

1,624. IN WHICH GAME DO YOU DROP DISCS INTO A VERTICAL GRID?

1,625. In a game of Battleship, how many ships does each player start the game with?

a. 4   b. 8

c. 5   d. 7

1,626. In Candyland, what happens when you land on a space with a black dot?

a. You lose the game

b. You lose a turn

c. You have to start over

d. You can advance one extra space

1,627. How many cards are in an Uno deck?

a. 52

b. 100

c. 108

d. 120

1,628. IN THE GAME OPERATION, WHAT IS THE PATIENT'S NAME?

1,629. True or false? The phrase "back to square one" probably comes from Snakes and Ladders.

1,630. In the game of Yahtzee, how many dice are used?

a. 3

b. 4

c. 5

d. 5

1,631. In the game of Risk, if there is a tie in the dice roll, which side wins?

a. The attacker

b. It's a tie, and they must reroll

c. The defender

d. Both

1,632. How many squares are on a checkerboard?
  a. 144
  b. 64
  c. 100
  d. All of the above

1,633. In chess, a king can be moved to safety next to a rook. What is this move called?
  a. Castling
  b. Fortifying
  c. Kinging
  d. Rooking

1,634. Where was backgammon created?
  a. India
  b. Persia
  c. Arabia
  d. China

1,635. TRUE OR FALSE? SCRABBLE CAN'T BE PLAYED IN THE CHINESE LANGUAGE.

TOUGH TRIVIA CHALLENGE

1,636. IN CLUE, WHAT DOES COLONEL MUSTARD SLEEP WITH UNDER HIS PILLOW?

1,637. In the game of Risk, what is the smallest number of units you need to have in a territory in order to attack?
  a. 1   b. 2   c. 3   d. 4

1,638. What is the largest room on the Clue board?
  a. The sitting room
  b. The ballroom
  c. The kitchen
  d. The hall

Answers: 1,624. Connect Four; 1,625. c; 1,626. b; 1,627. c; 1,628. Cavity Sam; 1,629. True; 1,630. d; 1,631. c; 1,632. d; 1,633. a; 1,634. b; 1,635. True; 1,636. A revolver; 1,637. b; 1,638. b.

Sports & Games • 183

1,639. In Stratego, which is the only piece that can't be killed by a bomb?

    a. Scout
    b. Marshall
    c. Miner
    d. Spy

▲▲▲▲▲▲▲▲▲▲▲▲▲▲▲▲

1,640. True or false? The game Operation was originally a different game called Death Valley

▲▲▲▲▲▲▲▲▲▲▲▲▲▲▲▲

1,641. In Scrabble, how many points is a Z worth?

1,642. True or false? In chess, the bishop can only move diagonally.

1,643. Chutes and Ladders is based on an old game from India called what?

    a. Snakes and Arrows
    b. Slings and Arrows
    c. Snakes and Ladders
    d. Chutes and Lutes

1,644. In the game of Yahtzee, how many points do you get for a Yahtzee after your first one?

    a. 40
    b. 50
    c. 60
    d. 100

▲▲▲▲▲▲▲▲▲▲▲▲▲▲▲▲

1,645. In the game of Risk, which continent is worth the most?

    a. Africa
    b. Europe
    c. Asia
    d. Australia

▲▲▲▲▲▲▲▲▲▲▲▲▲▲▲▲

1,646. Who moves first in a game of backgammon?

    a. The player who rolls the highest die score
    b. The players decide between them
    c. The player who rolls the lowest die score
    d. Whoever won the previous game

1,647. Chess probably originated in which country?
a. Japan   b. India
c. Egypt   d. Sumeria

▲▲▲▲▲▲▲▲▲▲▲▲▲▲

1,648. In backgammon, how many pieces does each player normally start with?
a. 10   b. 12   c. 15   d. 21

1,649. The game of dominoes probably originated where?
a. Spain   b. China
c. India   d. Turkey

▲▲▲▲▲▲▲▲▲▲▲▲▲▲▲▲▲▲▲▲▲▲▲▲▲▲

MATCH THE FOLLOWING GAMES WITH THE YEARS THEY WERE FIRST SOLD:

1,650. Trivial Pursuit	a. 1934
1,651. Operation	b. 1965
1,652. Boggle	c. 1963
1,653. Clue	d. 1981
1,654. Pictionary	e. 1972
1,655. Carcassonne	f. 1967
1,656. Sorry!	g. 1985
1,657. Catan	h. 1949
1,658. Battleship	i. 1995
1,659. Mouse Trap	j. 2000

Answers: 1,639. c; 1,640.True; 1,641. 10; 1,642.True; 1,643. c; 1,644. d; 1,645. c; 1,646. a; 1,647. b; 1,648. c; 1,649. b; 1,650. d; 1,651. b; 1,652. e; 1,653. h; 1,654. g; 1,655. j; 1,656. a; 1,657. i; 1,658. f; 1,659. c

1,660. "JENGA" IS THE SWAHILI WORD FOR WHAT?

1,661. Which of these is not a room in the standard, classic edition of Clue?

a. Lounge
b. Billiard Room
c. Spa
d. Conservatory

1,662. If you still have letter "Q" at the end of the game of Scrabble, how many points do you lose?

a. 5   b. 7
c. 10   d. 12

1,663. In a standard playing card deck, the King of hearts doesn't have what?

1,664. In the standard version of Catan, how many victory points do you need to win?

a. 4   b. 8   c. 10   d. 12

1,665. Where did dominoes first become popular in Europe in the eighteenth century?

a. Germany   b. France
c. Italy   d. Spain

1,666. In chess, when a pawn reaches the end of the board, what happens?

a. It has to turn around and come back
b. The player wins
c. The pawn is removed by the opponent
d. The pawn is "promoted" and becomes another piece

1,667. In the game of **Risk**, how many territories does Australia have?

   a. 3
   b. 5
   c. 4
   d. 2

1,668. What is the main goal of Stratego?

   a. The remove all you opponent's pieces
   b. To capture your opponent's flag
   c. To remove all your opponent's bombs
   d. To capture your opponent's Marshall

1,669. In Clue, what is the professor's last name?

   a. Berry
   b. Mustard
   c. Peacock
   d. Plum

1,670. True or false? The Game of Life was the only board game that Milton Bradley ever invented himself.

1,671. WHICH GAME USED COLORED MARBLES AND A STAR-SHAPED BOARD?

1,672. PARCHEESI ORIGINATES FROM WHERE?

1,673. In the game of Risk, for every three territories you have, how many armies do you get?

   a. 2
   b. 3
   c. 1
   d. 4

1,674. "Scrabble" comes from the Dutch word *schrabbelan*, which means what?
   a. To spell
   b. To speak loudly
   c. To claw or scrape
   d. To create

◆ ◆ ◆ ◆ ◆ ◆ ◆ ◆ ◆ ◆ ◆ ◆ ◆ ◆

1,675. How many squares are there on a Scrabble board?
   a. 144   b. 225
   c. 100   d. 196

1,676. What is another name for checkers?
   a. Discs
   b. Pentacles
   c. Coins
   d. Draughts

1,677. Which Egyptian game was checkers based on?
   a. Al-Azif
   b. Fox and Geese
   c. Alquerque
   d. Pharaohs

1,678. In Stratego, which piece is the only one that can move more than one square at a time?
   a. Lieutenant
   b. Marshall
   c. Flag
   d. Scout

◆ ◆ ◆ ◆ ◆ ◆ ◆ ◆ ◆ ◆ ◆ ◆ ◆ ◆

1,679. Which game has tricks, auctions, and grand slams?

◆ ◆ ◆ ◆ ◆ ◆ ◆ ◆ ◆ ◆ ◆ ◆ ◆ ◆

1,680. In the game of Chutes and Ladders, what do you land on that lets you move ahead?
   a. Arrow
   b. Chute
   c. Ladder
   d. Snake

◆ ◆ ◆ ◆ ◆ ◆ ◆ ◆ ◆ ◆ ◆ ◆ ◆ ◆

1,681. True or false? Originally, Scrabble didn't have a board and was just played with the tiles.

1,682. In the card game Freecell, which card do you need to start a foundation?

1,683. In dominoes, what does the word "downing" mean?
a. Losing the game
b. Putting down the first tile of the game
c. Blocking your opponent
d. Putting down the final tile of the game

1,684. In chess, how does one win?
a. By trapping the enemy king so it can't escape
b. By capturing the enemy king
c. By capturing the enemy queen
d. By eliminating all the opponent's pieces

1,685. In backgammon, where must you throw your dice?
a. On the left side of the board
b. On the table next to the board
c. On the right side of the board
d. Anywhere you like

◆◆◆◆◆◆◆◆◆◆◆◆◆◆

1,686. True or false?
In Stratego, only three pieces can kill the Marshall.

◆◆◆◆◆◆◆◆◆◆◆◆◆◆

TOUGH TRIVIA CHALLENGE

1,687. IN THE CARD GAME HEARTS, WHAT *IS* THE QUEEN OF SPADES CALLED?

Answers: 1,674. c; 1,675. b; 1,676. d; 1,677. c; 1,678. d; 1,679. Bridge; 1,680. c; 1,681. True; 1,682. Ace; 1,683. d; 1,684. a; 1,685. c; 1,686. True; 1,687. Black Lady or Black Maria

1,688. In Catan, what do you need to build roads?
a. Wood and concrete   b. Clay and stone
c. Wood and stone   d. Brick and wood

1,689. Standard checker pieces move how?
a. Backwards   b. Forward diagonally
c. Forward vertically   d. Sideways

1,690. In the card game Gin Rummy, how many cards does each player get?

1,691. In what year did its creators come up with the idea for Trivial Pursuit?
a. 1977   b. 1979   c. 1981   d. 1984

1,692. TRUE OR FALSE? THE GAME OF RISK WAS ORIGINALLY RELEASED IN GERMANY

1,693. The Game of Life, the first board game created by Milton Bradley, came out in what year?
a. 1900   b. 1875   c. 1860   d. 1890

1,694. In Candyland, what is the object of the game?
- a. To collect all the cards
- b. Be the first to get to the end
- c. Be the first to return to the start
- d. To eliminate your opponents

1,695. True or false? In chess, the rook is the weakest piece.

1,696. In what game would you draw an "Advance to Go" card?

1,697. In Clue, what is the red character's last name?
- a. Barry
- b. Redd
- c. Scarlet
- d. Rose

1,698. In Stratego, what is the name of the highest-ranking piece?
- a. Marshall
- b. Admiral
- c. General
- d. Colonel

1,699. WHICH CARD GAME HAS VERSIONS CALLED "SPIDER" AND "SCORPION"?

1,700. WHICH CARD GAME INCLUDES THE RARE BLACK LOTUS CARD?

Answers: 1,688. d; 1,689. b; 1,690. 10; 1,691. b; 1,692. False, it was first released in France; 1,693. c; 1,694. b; 1,695. False, the pawn is the weakest piece; 1,696. Monopoly; 1,697. c; 1,698. a; 1,699. Solitaire; 1,700. Magic: The Gathering

ABOUT APPLESAUCE PRESS

Good ideas ripen with time. From seed to harvest, Applesauce Press crafts books with beautiful designs, creative formats, and kid-friendly information on a variety of fascinating topics. Like our parent company, Cider Mill Press Book Publishers, our press bears fruit twice a year, publishing a new crop of titles each spring and fall.

Write to us at:
PO Box 454
Kennebunkport, ME 04046

Or visit us online at:
cidermillpress.com